Geneviève Jacques

Beyond Impunity

*An Ecumenical Approach
to Truth, Justice and
Reconciliation*

WCC Publications, Geneva

Cover design: Rob Lucas
Cover photo: André Jacques

ISBN 2-8254-1321-6

© 2000 WCC Publications, World Council of Churches,
150 route de Ferney, P.O. Box 2100,
1211 Geneva 2, Switzerland

Web site: http://www.wcc-coe.org

Printed in Switzerland

Table of Contents

v   Preface   *Konrad Raiser*

viii   Introduction   *Dwain Epps*

1   1. What Is Impunity?

15   2. Truth and Memory

34   3. Justice and Forgiveness

53   4. The Prospect of Reconciliation

Preface

Two recent events have brought the international discussion of impunity to a decisive turning point. The first was the decision by an intergovernmental conference in Rome in July 1998 to establish an International Court of Criminal Justice; the second was the ruling by the British law lords four months later that the former Chilean military ruler General Augusto Pinochet could legally be tried under foreign jurisdiction for crimes against humanity.

The question of impunity has been on the agenda of the World Council of Churches for some time. Already in 1996 the WCC published *Impunity: An Ethical Perspective*, edited by Charles Harper, who had been responsible for more than fifteen years for the Council's Human Rights Resources Office for Latin America. The six case studies in this book documented the struggle of Latin American human rights groups and churches against the official culture of silence which, under the guise of defending "national security", covered up the massive violations of human rights in that part of the world during the period of military dictatorship and protected those responsible from legal prosecution by way of amnesty laws.

The discussion took a new turn when the Truth and Reconciliation Commission was created in post-apartheid South Africa with the task of establishing a full picture "of the causes, nature and extent of the gross violations of human rights" committed during the thirty years since 1960. Similar commissions have been set up in a number of other countries, among which the commission in Guatemala is a particularly notable example. Later, the decision of the United Nations to establish two international tribunals to bring to trial those responsible for the atrocities in the former Yugoslavia and in Rwanda forced the issue of impunity out into the open.

The present study by Geneviève Jacques grows out of the ongoing ecumenical reflection supported by the WCC's Commission of the

Churches on International Affairs and drawing on the insights and experiences in many different situations. It provides a welcome introduction into the complex legal, political and human problems surrounding the issue of impunity and the efforts to establish and defend the rule of law in countries emerging from decades of oppressive rule or from devastating civil conflicts. Obviously, the judicial system faces limitations in the effort to determine responsibilities in situations of prolonged, massive violation of human rights and to respond to legitimate claims for justice on the part of the victims. But there is a growing public awareness that the granting or the de facto acceptance of impunity for those holding political, military or economic power erodes the very basis of the social order and helps to nurture a "culture of violence".

Significantly, however, this study goes beyond the purely legal and political aspects of impunity to explore the essential links between truth and memory, justice and reconciliation. Drawing especially on the experience of South Africa and Guatemala, Geneviève Jacques shows that one of the strongest driving forces of the struggle against impunity is the existential need of the victims to break out of a situation of silence, isolation, fear and falsehood, to know the truth, to recover a shared memory and thus to restore human dignity for the victims and accountability for the perpetrators. Without the intentional attempt to create a space where the stories of humiliation and suffering can be told, where the truth can emerge and collective remembrance be restored, the search for justice will continue to divide the community rather than re-establish relationships and contribute to a process of healing.

This obviously raises the question of the relationship between justice and reconciliation or forgiveness. This is addressed in the third part of the present study, which probably represents its most penetrating contribution. "Justice – the rule of law, respect for and obedience to the law – is the foundation of democratic society. It is essential to lasting peace within and between societies and nations. For the Christian, however, justice understood in purely legal terms is a step on the way to the more fundamental goal of reconciliation." Building again on the work of the Truth and Reconciliation Commission in South Africa, Geneviève Jacques introduces and unfolds the concept of "restorative justice", which is already finding wide acceptance in the ecumenical discussion. While it is important to prevent the call for reconciliation from weakening the commitment to justice, it must be recognized that justice and reconciliation are intimately connected and that forgiveness is part of the struggle for justice in the sense of re-establishing right relationships.

This book is thus a very significant contribution to the renewed discussion of the churches' potential role as agents of reconciliation.

It provides examples and suggestions of what churches can bring to that process of spiritual and moral, social and political transformation which will prepare the way for genuine reconciliation and help to build a culture of truthfulness and peace leading effectively beyond impunity.

Konrad Raiser

Introduction

The founders of the United Nations were painfully aware that the failure of the nations to learn the lessons of history had led repeatedly to barbarity, cruelty, widespread injustice and war in the early decades of the 20th century. They were determined to reverse this cycle by creating standards that would become universally accepted and followed. This determination echoes through the Preamble to the United Nations Charter:

> ...to save succeeding generations from the scourge of war..., and to reaffirm faith in fundamental human rights, in the dignity and worth of the human person, in the equal rights of men and women and of nations large and small, and to establish conditions under which justice and respect for the obligations arising from treaties and other sources of international law can be maintained, and to promote social progress and better standards of life in larger freedom..., and to practise tolerance and live together in peace, with one another as good neighbours...

A similar intention is expressed in the Universal Declaration of Human Rights, proclaimed by the United Nations General Assembly on 10 December 1948. Its provisions have been codified in international law through the International Human Rights Covenants and a host of other legally binding instruments:

> Whereas recognition of the inherent dignity and of the equal and inalienable rights of all members of the human family is the foundation of freedom, justice and peace in the world,
>
> Whereas disregard and contempt for human rights have resulted in barbarous acts which have outraged the conscience of mankind...

How is it then that in the last decade of the 20th century the present generation allowed itself to be victimized by terrible acts of genocide, ethnic cleansing and other massive crimes against humanity? How can such practices as systematic torture, disappearance, forced movements of populations – applied by military dictatorships in many countries during the 1970s and 1980s – continue until today, even though they have been explicitly outlawed by international law? Why has the world so stubbornly refused to learn the lessons of even the recent past, and allowed obvious conflicts to explode, one after another, into new, brutal wars?

The reasons are complex. But many victims of past atrocities have become convinced that among the causes of present-day atrocities is the fact that many of the perpetrators of past crimes have not been held to account for their acts, and that the truth about their crimes often remains hidden. How can we learn from the past if we are denied such truth? How can victims live alongside those whom they know to be responsible for atrocities, yet who have neither acknowledged their guilt nor given sign of repentance?

Too often, the response is, "Forget the past, let the dead bury the dead, live and let live, turn your eyes to the future." This simplistic answer, so easily offered by those who have something to hide, has no healing power. It leaves no room for reconciliation, victims say. Unless the truth is told, unless the criminals are held accountable, or unless those directly responsible and their accomplices confess their guilt, ask for forgiveness and give concrete signs of repentance, there can be no justice and therefore no healing of society.

Can humanity then do no more than repeat the errors of the past, trapped in cycles of retributive violence? Christians cannot accept such a fatalistic view of history. They look for transformation. They believe that God intends to right the scales of justice, that through Christ and the work of the Holy Spirit humanity *can* change course. Real justice, real repentance and real reconciliation *are* possible. There *is* hope for "succeeding generations".

A new consciousness of the unacceptable is emerging after a century that witnessed so many atrocities. From Latin America to the Great Lakes region of Africa, from Germany to Japan, from South Africa to the former communist countries of Europe, from Cambodia to Bosnia, from the United States of America to Australia, societies are asking the haunting questions which time has not erased from memory. In many places Christians in the ecumenical movement have taken a powerful lead in helping societies to work through these questions. What they discover is that the issues lie deep in history, and most often cross borders. They are beginning – spiritually, intellectually and through practical actions – to form themselves into a movement against impunity, for justice, for reconciliation, and thus for the holistic peace Christ came to give those who choose to follow him.

This book is written to help Christians and their churches to confront the complicated issues involved, joining hands across the boundaries of race, class, ethnicity, national belonging and even history in order to seek a new way. It is intended more to help readers to frame the questions emerging out of their own experiences and in their own places than to give ready solutions. It offers examples of some movements in which Christians have engaged with secular counterparts and people of other faiths to work together for real change. The aim is to encourage, broaden and strengthen a common awareness in the ecumenical movement that will enable the churches to take a clear and committed stance on these issues, both at home and internationally.

We begin by defining the meaning of impunity and illustrating the evolution of awareness of this phenomenon in relation to the events of the latter part of this century. We then turn to the ethical challenges and Christian responsibilities that are central to the struggle to put a stop to impunity. Finally, we point to some of the resources available for further study of this issue. A considerable body of ecumenical reflection is emerging on truth, justice, repentance, forgiveness, reconciliation and the healing of society, including several books published by the World Council of Churches.

This is a "work in progress". We hope readers will be stimulated to add their own stories, reflections, experiences and practical approaches, and to share these with the World Council of Churches so that they can be made more widely available to those similarly engaged in different parts of the world.

Dwain Epps

1. What Is Impunity?

Understanding the importance of impunity

The word "impunity" comes from the Latin *impunitas*, "absence of punishment". Until recently, it has been used almost exclusively in legal contexts to designate the process by which individuals are freed from any penalty for their illegal or criminal acts.

The notion of impunity began to take on a broader social meaning in Latin America in the aftermath of the massive violations of human rights committed in the name of the doctrine of national security by military dictatorships throughout South and Central America during the 1970s and 1980s. As these authoritarian regimes began to give way to democratically elected governments, many military establishments decreed an amnesty for all those who held positions of responsibility in the outgoing regimes. The newly elected parliaments of these still very fragile democracies sometimes ratified these decrees or adopted amnesty laws of their own, fearing that former military rulers, who retained powerful means, might try to overthrow the new democratic institutions if any legal action were taken against them.

In every case, such amnesty decrees or laws evoked massive protests, especially from victims of torture and the family members of persons who had been murdered or caused to "disappear" under the former, unashamedly cruel military regime. The victims' voices against impunity were amplified by civil society organizations that had defended human rights during the time of the dictatorships. In many of these organizations the churches, both Catholic and Protestant, had played and continued to play a central role. They energetically condemned impunity for the gross and systematic violations of human rights committed by the military and those associated with their rule as morally, politically and socially unacceptable.

More than twenty years later, popular mobilization against impunity is as strong as ever in the Southern Cone (Chile, Argentina, Uruguay) and has spread to the Andean region (Peru, Colombia) and Central America (El Salvador, Guatemala). Everywhere, the victims have remained determined that seeing truth and justice prevail is an essential precondition for national reconciliation, and a key element in the struggle for human dignity and against social exclusion in an age of globalization.

We shall see how risky this struggle against impunity in Latin America and elsewhere is and what enormous courage it has required. Societies remain deeply divided along political, ideological and philosophical lines. Important sectors remain convinced that military rule was necessary to "stop the spread of communism". Others, fearing a return of military rule, hesitate to stir up old animosities at a time when a semblance of democracy prevails. Still others insist that without justice there can be no basis for a stable democracy.

The case of the former Chilean dictator General Augusto Pinochet has highlighted the legal, political and social complexities. Pinochet was arrested in London, where he had travelled for medical treatment, at the request of authorities in Spain, where a court was seeking his appearance on charges related to his rule. Both Pinochet and the government of Chile protested vigorously. A condition of his handing over power earlier had been that he be made senator-for-life, precisely in order to guarantee his impunity. After extended consideration, the British law lords ruled on 25 November 1998 that the former dictator could legally be tried for crimes against humanity under a foreign jurisdiction. This historic decision marked the first time that a former head of state was found prosecutable abroad (though others acting under military authority had been previously been arrested and prosecuted). As the French daily *Le Monde* put it:

> Whatever ultimately comes of it, the 25th of November 1998 will always be an important date in our history, for the simple reason that on that day fear began to change sides. Fear, the means by which all dictatorships govern, the ultimate weapon of all forms of state terrorism, is no longer reserved for the victims. For dictators this marks the transition from the age of impunity to the age of illegality.[1]

Defining the term

The legal definition of impunity includes three key elements: the offence committed, the perpetrator of the offence and the requirements of justice.[2]

Regarding the nature of the offence, human rights organizations and lawyers tend to agree that impunity has to do with *serious human rights violations*, including crimes considered "serious" under international law (war crimes, crimes against humanity, genocide, torture) and "gross and systematic violations" of civil and political rights and economic, social and cultural rights.

With respect to the perpetrator, the prevailing position has been to stress *official political responsibility* – actions of "agents of the state, or of individuals acting under the orders or with the complicity, connivance, approval or encouragement of the authorities".[3] However, more recent discussion has also considered extending the definition to include non-state groups – for example, paramilitary or para-police groups – as perpetrators.

Justice requires that *the perpetrators of human rights violations be brought to account* through a process which includes investigation of the facts, indictment, trial, sentencing and determination of reparation for the victim of the offence. By contrast, impunity means, in the words of UN special rapporteur on impunity Louis Joinet,

> the impossibility, *de jure* or *de facto*, of bringing the perpetrators of human rights violations to account – whether in criminal, civil, administrative or disciplinary proceedings – since they are not subject to any inquiry that might lead to their being accused, arrested, tried and, if found guilty, convicted, and to reparations being made to their victims.[4]

The "culture of impunity"

While these legal discussions raise technical issues, one does not have to be a lawyer to understand the legal, political and ethical implications of impunity for the victims or for society as a whole, especially when ongoing and systematic human rights violations have occurred. Yet both the direct victims of violations and society at large may have their awareness of the nature of the problem and of the possibility of doing something about it dulled when the practice of impunity becomes routine and ingrained over time. In such cases we can identify a "culture of impunity", which needs to be overcome.

A culture of impunity points to something wrong with the system as a whole, with its rules and with its codes of behaviour. In such a culture, the problem is not simply one of deviant acts by certain individuals. The legal system itself is systematically co-opted, and impunity becomes a "normal" attribute of power. Certain people consider themselves to be above the law, above morality, unaccountable to anyone for any of their actions, no matter how serious. A Rwandan human rights worker summed up the situation in his country before the 1994 genocide in these words: "In Rwanda impunity had become normal – a culture in which evil acts could be committed with no possibility of prosecution." Impunity had become the norm.

The struggle against impunity is an integral part of the defence and promotion of human rights in all situations. It becomes a priority human rights concern in societies struggling to reconstitute themselves after long periods of conflict, dictatorship or anti-democratic regimes, for under such circumstances the protection impunity affords perpetrators of past crimes is a principal barrier to national reconciliation.

The threat to democracy and society

Impunity denies the principle of equality before the law, one of the foundations of democracy and the rule of law. Impunity destroys the confidence of citizens in the authority and role of the state and in its ability to protect their rights. When those in power are permitted to do anything, it gives currency to the perverse idea that everyone is permitted to settle accounts as they wish with no respect for the law. Impunity thus engenders social frustration, despair, resignation and apathy, while feeding aggressiveness, violence, the collapse of moral restraints and the rejection of the values on which a cohesive society relies. It fosters a culture of violence devoid of ethical principles.

According to Paz Rojas, a Chilean neuropsychiatrist,

> the continuance of impunity produces patterns of psychological disorder capable of causing mental disturbances comparable to, if not more serious than, torture. When the responsibility of criminals is suppressed, the trauma resulting from a crime, which remains hidden in the realm of injustice, remains a deep, open wound in the personal and social life of the victims.[5]

The silence imposed through impunity locks all the victims, both direct and indirect, into their suffering and despair. Healing and social rehabilitation are made difficult if not impossible. In the absence of any form of justice, victims cannot break free of their hatred and desire for revenge. At the same time, the perpetrators too – whether they remain unaware of, unrepentant for or burdened with their crimes – cannot recover their human dignity by acknowledging their guilt and paying their debt to society.

Impunity represents the triumph of falsehood, silence and oblivion. It violates and poisons the memory of individuals and of communities. Ideologies and doctrines which led to past criminal acts are neither condemned nor questioned; consequently, they hang like a sword of Damocles over the heads of the victims and society as a whole. Thus impunity makes true reconciliation in society impossible. By suppressing any meaningful contact between victims and those responsible for their suffering, it prevents any restoration of relationships, both between individuals and between groups.

New awareness of an age-old problem

> There is a long and bitter history of impunity in Africa. Serious, mass, systematic human rights violations, in the form of slavery and colonialism, have been completely concealed beneath the cloak of impunity.[6]

Impunity is not a new phenomenon. Individuals and groups in power have gone unpunished for serious human rights violations throughout the history of most of the world's peoples.

Shadrack Gutto, a Kenyan university professor, argues that the impunity regarding their crimes in Africa from which the European colonial powers benefited has seriously diminished the moral authority of international human rights declarations in African eyes. This has permitted and even encouraged the governments of many African states, once they became independent, to perpetuate a culture of impunity for human rights violations committed or supported by the state and its authorities.

Africa of course is only one contemporary case in point. It has been suggested that the failure of the international community to acknowledge the 1915 Armenian genocide was very substantially to blame for the Jewish Holocaust in Europe a quarter-century later. The continuing refusal of the Turkish state to acknowledge responsibility for this atrocity deeply affects the dispersed Armenian people still today. This hurt is passed from generation to generation, along with the insistent demand that both Turkey and the world officially recognize the truth of the genocide and name those responsible. Short of this, the unreconciled memory of the martyrs will remain for the Armenian people a continuing source of deep pain and conflict.

Because of the Nuremberg and Tokyo trials, one cannot speak of impunity for the principal official perpetrators of the atrocities committed in Europe and Asia during the second world war. But this does not prevent the victims from continuing to demand to know the truth and to trace the chain of responsibility for some of the sinister human rights violations committed at that time – among them the sexual slavery of "comfort women" in Asia, the confiscation of Jewish funds and property in Europe, the forced labour by civilians, the genocidal acts against the Roma people. Though apologies have been offered in a number of cases, states have generally been unable or unwilling to assume the burden of their predecessors' crimes.

Two of the 20th century's most costly tragedies in terms of human life have occurred in its concluding decade – the Rwandan genocide and the succession of wars in the former Yugoslavia. Each is at least in part a consequence of impunity. In Rwanda both Hutus and Tutsis remember and refer back to waves of unpunished crimes by the one against the other in various periods of their post-independence history. The peoples of the former Yugoslavia carry memories of brutalities at the hands of others for at least five centuries; despite all that has occurred since then, they still hark back to ancient hurts and unresolved territorial claims to fuel their present-day conflicts.

The Middle East also remains troubled by centuries of conquests and unresolved issues that go even further back than the Ottoman empire and the crusades undertaken by the Western church.

Readers will no doubt be able to identify many other situations in which there are poignant and important reminders that impunity, with its denial of the verifiable truth and refusal to allow the healing of memories, ticks away like a time bomb in the midst of societies. One could mention French nuclear testing in Polynesia, intentional experimentation by the US government on its own armed forces to determine the effects of chemical and nuclear weapons, the tragedy of the deadly chemical accident at the Union Carbide plant in Bhopal, India, the plight of native and indigenous peoples all over the world.

In sum, the conscience of humankind on the threshold of the third millennium remains haunted by mass and systematic crimes which have escaped judgment and which leave in the memory of the traumatized victims and peoples a permanent scar which time cannot remove, so long as there remains a feeling that a great injustice has not been put right.

Over the centuries philosophers have in different ways stated the dilemma: those who are unable to learn the lessons of the past are destined to repeat its errors. When the present is unworthy of the past, the future will soon take its revenge.

Since issues of impunity have poisoned human relations for so long, why has it come to light with such force now? How can we explain this new international awareness that it is imperative to take up this issue seriously today?

As noted in the introduction, more than anything else the ecumenical movement has been made conscious of this by the courageous and determined struggles of victims and their families, nurtured by the human rights movement, in which the churches in many parts of the world have played a significant role. Out of that movement has come an awareness of the centrality of the law and international standards; and through this movement dynamic forces in civil society have joined together across confessional, ideological and other lines in demanding a more determined approach to eradicating this blight from the history of peoples.

The origins of this development lie in events in Latin America. In the early 1970s, when military dictatorships ruled in triumph on that continent, associations of political prisoners' families, human rights organizations and movements in the church were mobilized at national and international levels to campaign for an amnesty for political prisoners, as a symbol of freedom in opposition to the arbitrary power being exercised by the military.

Ironically, in the 1980s it was the dictators on their way out who seized on the theme of amnesty for self-protection. The sole object of amnesty laws passed in most of these countries was thus to legalize impunity for the perpetrators of the most serious violations, such as disappearances, torture and massacres, committed under the military governments during the darkest days of the repression. With an appeal to the "greater good" of national reconciliation, decrees were issued or laws adopted to draw a line under the past, preventing any legal investigation into the facts of human rights violations and thus protecting their perpetrators from having to answer to justice. The most egregious of the many cases in point were Chile, Argentina and Uruguay.

Such decrees and legislation were vociferously condemned as morally and politically scandalous by associations of victims' families, human rights workers and the churches. All have been outraged by the contempt shown for the victims, particularly in the cases of the disappeared, and deeply concerned about the danger these violations presented for fledgling new democracies.

Impunity and international law

Thanks to networks of solidarity, in which the World Council of Churches has played a significant role, the cries against impunity echoed beyond national frontiers. In 1991 the United Nations Commission on Human Rights directed its Sub-Commission on Prevention of Discrimination and Protection of Minorities to conduct a study of impunity in order to establish "a set of principles for the protection and promotion of human rights through action to combat impunity". The study was divided into two parts: one on the violation of civil and political rights, entrusted to Louis Joinet, and the other on the violation of economic, social and cultural rights, entrusted to El Hadji Guisse. Their final reports were submitted to the Sub-Commission in August 1997.[7]

Many hope that this initial work will lead to the elaboration of enforceable international instruments to eradicate the most extreme forms of impunity, but history shows that this is likely to be a protracted process. Following the adoption of the Universal Declaration of Human Rights in 1948, it took 18 years to make its provisions enforceable through the drafting and approval of the International Covenants on Human Rights, and two more decades to obtain a sufficient number of ratifications by states to put oversight mechanisms in place.

Other official steps that move in a positive direction on impunity have been taken in recent years. One was the creation by the United Nations Security Council of the two international tribunals on the former Yugoslavia (1993) and on Rwanda (1994) to try and punish persons in those two countries who were responsible for crimes against humanity and acts of "ethnic cleansing" and genocide. Many have questioned the motivation behind these Security Council decisions and the effectiveness of the two tribunals. Were they primarily a way for some powerful states to cover up their own failure to act in a timely way to prevent or arrest the tragedies in those two countries, just at the moment when their peoples most needed external help? Will these tribunals in fact receive the resources and develop the will to fulfil their mandates and prepare the ground for national reconciliation within these nations? Will they be kept sufficiently free of partisan political pressures to retain their judicial objectivity and prosecute all those, from any side, who committed crimes?

Nevertheless, limited though they may be, the very existence of these international tribunals sends a clear signal that certain particularly serious crimes under international law cannot go unpunished, and that the international community will not remain passive or indifferent to such injustice. The momentum resulting from the creation of these tribunals – and the debates which took place at the time – was a strong impulse towards realization of the long-held hope that an independent international body be formed to address such matters. A United Nations diplomatic conference in Rome in 1998 adopted, to the applause of delegates, the Statute of Rome for an International Criminal Court, despite the resistance of one or two especially powerful delegations, which sought to water down its powers and weaken its independence.

An effective international system of criminal justice, competent to punish crimes against humanity on the basis of universally recognized principles, will not be firmly established for a long time yet, but there is wide agreement that an historic step has been taken. The way is now open to roll back the rule of impunity for the perpetrators of the most serious crimes. What is important now is that organizations involved in the defence of human rights, including churches, keep up popular pressure to make sure that this question remains on the international agenda, that all states ratify the statute of the international court and that such an instrument be put firmly in place.

The need for change

Even when such an international court is established, it will remain no more than a symbol in the struggle against impunity if it is not accompanied by a broad international effort at education and awareness-building which can lead to a change of heart in public opinion and among decision-makers. This is a daunting challenge.

Nowhere is this clearer than in recent cases of countries in "transition". In the last decade of the 20th century, many nations have thrown off the shackles of dictatorship, apartheid and totalitarian rule. Often this has come through or given rise to terrible civil wars or international conflicts, characterized by massive human rights violations against civilian populations. In all these cases, new governments have had to confront the dreadful legacy of the past and the question of what to do about those primarily responsible for such crimes. The problem is compounded when political transition has been achieved through negotiations which required accepting elements of compromise with those who formerly held power (South Africa, El Salvador, Guatemala, Bosnia) or when former military rulers and institutions retain substantial power behind the scenes of constitutional democracies (Chile, Argentina, Uruguay, Cambodia, Indonesia).

The choices facing new civilian governments are often excruciatingly complex and difficult. A decision to prosecute former rulers and their accomplices risks the danger of a new military coup d'état and terrible reprisals. For the sake of stability, is it not better to grant amnesty, to accept impunity in the hope that "time will heal all wounds"? On the other hand, what price will society have to pay for applying the logic of oblivion and cheap "forgiveness"?

The issue of the passage of time is certainly not unimportant. It is understandable that democratic governments which are still precarious and threatened from within do not wish to make the fight against impunity the first battle they wage. But history shows the argument often advanced by governments that building a peaceful society for the future is incompatible with righting the injustices of the past to be an illusion in the long term. Peoples who bear the memory of past suffering and injustice are not prepared to open a new chapter of history before the previous chapter has been read and its lessons learned.

The declaration and programme of action adopted by the UN World Conference on Human Rights in Vienna in 1993 attests to the significant change of heart within the international community to which this dilemma is leading and to a new awareness of how important the struggle against impunity is for the healing of the traumas of both nations and individuals:

> The World Conference on Human Rights views with concern the issue of impunity of perpetrators of human rights violations, and supports the efforts of the Commission on Human Rights and the Sub-Commission on Prevention

of Discrimination and Protection of Minorities to examine all aspects of the issue.[8]

The problem of "the impossibility, *de jure* or *de facto,* of bringing the perpetrators of human rights violations to account" is not confined to the tragic situations cited above. It is a burning question within nearly every country where impunity has been granted to people whose hold on power has made them virtually untouchable under the law.

The World Council of Churches' "Peace to the City" campaign, part of its Programme to Overcome Violence, highlighted the increasing refusal of new coalitions of civil society, business and government to accept the granting of impunity to agents of the state who have committed serious crimes (torture, murder) against "undesirables" like street children, the homeless, foreigners, prostitutes or other people who have been pushed to the margins of society. "Security" is increasingly rejected as a rationale for injustice and the violation of human rights. "Official" violence, carried out by those sworn to respect the law, is increasingly being condemned by those who abhor violence in all its forms.

In the face of "cultures" of impunity, silence, injustice and civic irresponsibility, more and more people are speaking out and refusing to forget. There is a growing call by victims and human rights defenders – but also ordinary citizens – for "memory work" to be done by society as a whole. The search for truth, the exercise of the "right to know" and the need for justice are being recognized as much more than an academic exercise, an end in itself, but rather as essential to the very existence of human society. For unless steps are taken to restore the dignity of the victims and open the way for reconciliation through repentance and forgiveness, the atrocities of the past are almost certainly to be repeated. Increasingly, people are taking to heart the famous words attributed to Martin Niemöller:

First they came for the communists
And I did not speak out –
Because I was not a communist.

Then they came for the socialists
And I did not speak out –
Because I was not a socialist.

Then they came for the trade unionists
And I did not speak out –
Because I was not a trade unionist.

Then they came for the Jews
And I did not speak out –
Because I was not a Jew.

Then they came for me –
And there was no one left
To speak out for me.

The present generation is making new efforts to strip away the cloak of social or cultural acceptability from injustice and crimes of all sorts. For the exercise of power is not limited to that of the state. Other powers have long been beyond the reach of the law, with the benevolent complicity of state authorities.

As dramatically illustrated in testimonies gathered during the Ecumenical Decade – Churches in Solidarity with Women, patriarchal power in the home is one such form.[9] While violence against women in the home and in the community still goes largely unpunished in many countries, here too times are changing. Though there is still a long way to go before its defeat can be celebrated, some very important steps are being taken, both internationally and in national legislatures, towards recognizing and condemning such crimes committed in the private sphere. Thanks to the courage and determination of women's organizations, impunity for the perpetrators of violence against women is no longer a given everywhere.

Something similar is happening regarding those responsible for mass violations of economic, social and cultural rights. While such violations are by no means new in human history, the globalization of the free-market economy has given financial and economic power a kind of anonymity which often allows both government and corporate economic decision-makers to operate with total impunity, considering themselves responsible only for balancing budgets or making profit. As they become aware that their actions are leading to increasing environmental degradation, poverty, unemployment, economic exclusion and misery, many take refuge behind the old military argument: "I was only acting under orders." But here, too, victims of the violation of their rights and those of future generations have begun to protest for justice. Farmers organizations, for example, have begun to link arms across national and regional borders to protest the policies of bodies like the World Trade Organization which rob them of control over markets, and eventually of their rights to the land as a source of livelihood.

The Jubilee 2000 movement has drawn particular attention to how people's economic rights are being violated through the manipulation of debt, especially in the poorest countries. The WCC's eighth assembly (Harare 1998) gave voice to these concerns:

> The diversion of resources from impoverished peoples in debtor countries to rich Western creditors is a violation of human rights. Furthermore, the

impunity with which creditors are able to impose such policies is a travesty of justice. Children and women are forced to bear the full costs of debt repayment through reductions in health, sanitation, and clean water programmes.[10]

In the majority of cases, the victims of such systematic attacks on their basic rights do not have access to the truth about their situation, nor to justice or reparation. Here again, a long road remains to be travelled before rules can be shaped and enforced which can roll back impunity for economic crimes. But it is urgent to act, as the WCC assembly said, for the "establishment of an independent, transparent arbitration process for debt cancellation, and ethical lending and borrowing policies".

The role of the churches

Speaking at a WCC consultation, Argentine Methodist Bishop Aldo Etchegoyen offered a vivid illustration of how difficult and even dangerous the struggle against impunity can be for the churches which find themselves in the midst of complex and critical situations which call for courage and clear thinking:

> As often happens, the political, economic and military authorities turn to the religious authorities to justify their actions in relation to impunity. The granting of pardon is the political-legal instrument for implementing impunity; its theological justification is forgiveness...
>
> Religious leaders [in Argentina], Christians and others, were invited by a senior government official to form the National Commission for Peace... Of course, an initiative of this kind is important...; yet some of us had the suspicion that this whole programme was part of a political-religious manoeuvre... A few weeks before the decree granting pardon, we received a visit from a government official with a carefully prepared theological document linking forgiveness and pardon, which we were supposed to sign for the sake of peace.
>
> Some signed, many others did not. And why not? Because there were strong theological reasons that prevented us from putting pen to paper. The document offered pardon/forgiveness without repentance and without revealing what had happened to the thousands of people who had been tortured and murdered... I would have signed that document produced by the government if there had been any mention of repentance by the military, any admission of the truth about what had happened to the thousands of people who disappeared. How could I have signed... behind the backs of the mothers and grandmothers of the Plaza de Mayo, representing the families that have suffered so much grief?

To this theological and ethical challenge many in society are looking to the churches and Christian communities for an answer, as well as for support in their own very existential dilemmas. To give a response, both in theory and in practice, requires both humility and at the same time great courage – just as it took courage for the mothers and grandmothers of the disappeared in Argentina, whom the authorities regarded as insane, and for their sisters in Chile, Uruguay, Guatemala, Lebanon and Algeria, to go on obstinately demanding to know the truth about what had become of their children, grandchildren or husbands. It took courage for Korean and other Asian women abused and humiliated as sexual slaves by the Japanese imperial army during the second world war to struggle for decades to obtain official acknowledgment of guilt and reparations from those responsible. And it takes courage every day for all the men and women who refuse to give in and accept the unacceptable, who join together so that truth may triumph over falsehood or oblivion, justice and the equality of all before the law may be respected, and the poisoned roots that the culture of impunity has put down in their societies may be weeded out.

Christians and churches have been present in many of these struggles. From early on, they have stood alongside the victims in many societies, offering not only solace but also theological understanding and practical assistance. Some years ago, the WCC published a book which gathered together the witness and reflections on impunity by churches in six of the most dramatically affected Latin American countries in order to share their insights and pastoral experiences with the wider ecumenical movement.[11] A number of works from South Africa have detailed the churches' remarkable role there in promoting, creating and leading the Truth and Reconciliation Commission after the fall of the apartheid regime.[12]

Lamentably, not all churches or Christian communities have been so engaged, either for lack of awareness of the nature of the problem or, even more sadly, out of complicity themselves with those responsible for massive violations of human rights. In either case, the absence or silence of the churches with respect to the poisonous impact of impunity on society can have grievous consequences.

NOTES

[1] *Le Monde*, 27 Nov. 1998.

[2] Cf. Jose Burneo, "Amnistie et Impunité", Lyons, Human Rights Institute, 1996.

[3] Alejandro Artucio, in a paper presented to the international conference "Non à l'impunité, Oui à la justice", Geneva, Nov. 1992.

[4] Louis Joinet, "Issues of Impunity for the Perpetrators of (Civil and Political) Human Rights Violations", final report to the UN Sub-Commission for the Prevention of Discrimination and the Protection of Minorities, 49th session, Aug. 1997, E/CN.4/Sub.2/1997/20.

[5] Paz Rojas, "An Approach to the Medical-Psychological Consequences of Impunity for the Person", a paper presented (in Spanish) to the international seminar on impunity, Santiago, Chile, Dec. 1996.

[6] Shadrack Gutto, *Human and People's Rights for the Oppressed*, Lund, Sweden, Lund U.P., 1993, p. 57.

7 Cf. Joinet, *op. cit.;* for the final report by El Hadji Guisse, cf. E/CN.4/Sub.2/1997/8.

8 Final Document of the Vienna conference, A/CONF.157/23/ §91.

9 Among other resources, see Aruna Gnanadason, Musimbi Kanyoro and Lucy Ann McSpadden, eds, *Women, Violence and Nonviolent Change*, Geneva, WCC, 1996.

10 Diane Kessler, ed., *Together on the Way: Official Report of the Eighth Assembly of the WCC*, Geneva, WCC, 1999, p. 180.

11 Charles Harper, ed., *Impunity – An Ethical Perspective: Six Case Studies from Latin America*, Geneva, WCC, 1996.

12 Cf. in particular Russel Botman and Robin Petersen, eds, *To Remember and To Heal: Theological and Psychological Reflections on Truth and Reconciliation*, Cape Town, Human and Rousseau, 1996.

2. Truth and Memory

There remains an experience of incomparable value. We have for once learned to see the great events of world history from below, from the perspective of the outcasts, the suspects, the maltreated, the powerless, the oppressed, the reviled – in short, from the perspective of those who suffer.[1]

Dietrich Bonhoeffer,
from his cell in a Nazi prison in 1942

Our relationship to truth

To seek the truth, to know the truth, to tell the truth – for those who have endured the dark times of repression or conflict this is the first requirement, a vital, existential need.

For all those trying to live with a painful past which has left deep wounds in body and mind – for the immediate victims, for their families or survivors and for society as a whole – relating to the truth has both personal and collective aspects:

– *the need to break out of silence, isolation, fear and falsehood:* there is a need to tell the story of what has been experienced, and a thirst to know and to understand what really happened, why and how;
– *the need to establish historical clarity:* there is a need to see the truth revealed about events which have wounded individuals and society, and to see history interpreted in a way which names the deeds that were done, the reasons why they were done and who was responsible;
– *the need to restore memory:* there is a need to recover or establish a shared memory which is intelligible to everyone, in order to be able to envisage a different future in full knowledge of the destructive effects of past violations and humiliations.

If our relation to the truth has been broken or denied, for example by the granting of impunity to those whom we know from personal experience to be guilty, how will it be possible to restore or establish relationships of trust between individuals or groups?

Though expressed in various ways in different political and cultural contexts, the demand for the truth seems to be a constant in human societies. Today this demand or expectation on the part of victims is being taken up ever more widely by a public indignant over the human rights violations reported by the media. Even if the information broadcast is incomplete and often biased, it is more and more difficult to claim that "we didn't know". This emotional reaction to pictures or eye-witness accounts creates an awareness, which is expressed in demands for the whole truth to be told about tragic events.

Breaking the silence – the need to tell one's story

> There are crimes which must not be forgotten, victims whose suffering cries out not so much to be avenged as to be told.[2]

Every healing process begins with a time for speaking and listening, so that the victims can break out of the isolation and shame imposed by those who have wounded them, so that they can escape from their obsessive fear, so that they can recover their capacity to live in relationship with others, with people who are able to hear them. This is especially important in cases of torture and rape.

> "Scream as loud as you want; no one will hear you," torture victims in apartheid jails were often told by tormentors who were confident that knowledge of their crimes would never go beyond the cell walls. The defeat of the apartheid regime offers the opportunity for the suppressed anguish of these victims to be heard. "Now there is a chance for the whole world to hear the victims scream..." People must be allowed to tell their stories. The nation is obliged to hear them. It is in the encounter of telling, hearing and understanding that the reconciliation process can begin.[3]

All those who have the task of accompanying victims or survivors – doctors, psychologists, social workers, priests or pastors – agree on the crucial importance of this stage of speaking and listening, this time for allowing that part of the truth which every victim carries within himself or herself to be expressed.

This is a painful and difficult process, which some persons cannot or will not undertake on their own if the source of the pain is too recent, or if those around them are deaf to it. Why make the effort to remember and to talk about the pain if it only means torturing oneself anew by bringing to the surface stories, feelings and images that hurt? Can anyone hear? Who will understand?

Psychological and spiritual accompaniment is usually necessary to allow these memories to be expressed. Space is required – a space in which the victim can come to rely on a relationship of trust and real attention before crossing the threshold of his or her own silence to tell the story. This can be done individually with a qualified care-giver, or in a specialized trauma-counselling centre. It can also be done collectively within a community in a "speaking group".

> When I listen to others' stories, I am invited to move out of the subjectivity of my own story into another realm of thinking and acting. The same is true for others when I tell my story... Indeed, it is only when we refuse to listen to another story that our own story becomes ideological, that is, a closed system incapable of hearing the truth.[4]

In local communities in South Africa, a number of initiatives of this sort have developed on the fringes of the national process begun by the Truth and Reconciliation Commission. One such place, the Institute of Healing of Memories in Cape Town, has developed a methodology for sharing stories and accompanying persons through "healing of memories workshops".

> Essentially, each workshop is an individual and collective journey of exploring the effects of the apartheid years. The emphasis is on dealing with these issues at an emotional, psychological and spiritual level, rather than an intellectual one.
>
> The workshops provide a unique opportunity to experience and relate our individual journey, while sharing with others in theirs. Time is given for individual reflection, creative exercises and opportunities to share in a small group. There is also some reflection on the common themes that come up in such a journey – such as anger, hope, hatred, joy, isolation, endurance – and a discovery of the depths of common humanity we share. The workshop reaches its climax in the creation of a liturgy/celebration (including readings, poetry, dance, song, prayers, etc.) which provides a sense of completion to the workshop.

The difficulty and pain of telling one's story

For the victims of crimes against humanity and for those who come face to face with their effects, with actions intended to destroy the very worth and dignity of human beings, the pain is sometimes almost impossible to express and the account of it almost impossible to receive.

This was the experience of a great many of those who survived concentration camps at the end of the second world war. Many felt an intense need to speak, to write, to witness, to expose the horror and to pay homage to their companions who did not come back, so that, hearing them, the world would cry "Never again!" and use their words in a process of preventive education.

> "I wanted so much to speak," one victim remembers, "so many things to tell. Nobody wanted to hear about it. Some said, 'You have suffered so much, it

isn't worthwhile to talk about it.' But this wasn't so much to protect me as to protect themselves. So I stopped."[5]

Many women and men who have survived the hell of collective massacres, organized rapes, torture chambers or prison camps speak of this tension between the need on the one hand to tell and to be heard, and the difficulty on the other hand of telling and thus being exposed. The two testimonies that follow illustrate this. One comes from a member of the French resistance who escaped from the concentration camps, the other from a Moroccan poet who was imprisoned and tortured for his commitment to the defence of human rights.

The difficulty of recounting the unimaginable
During the first few days after we got back [from the concentration camps], I think we were all truly delirious. We wanted, at last, to speak and be heard. We are told that our physical appearance alone was quite eloquent. But we had just come back, bringing with us our memory, our experience which was so alive; we had a frantic desire to tell it just as it was. However, from the very first days it seemed impossible to us to overcome the distance, the distance we were discovering between the language available to us, and that experience... As soon as we started talking about it, we found ourselves suffocating. Even to our own selves, that which we had to tell was beginning to seem unimaginable.[6]

The pain of telling
Those who have experienced that ordeal of torture in their flesh and their consciousness can speak of it only with enormous difficulty. In speaking of that experience, they feel as though they are stripping themselves naked. Each of us experiences and interiorizes personal suffering in his or her own way... In the status of victim there is no respite, and one is not shielded from certain perversions. A victim never fails to arouse a kind of pity – is it not so? – or at best a sort of compassion which can sometimes wound the pride, even the dignity of the person. And then, can one always find partners for a conversation? Are there not sometimes, among them, persons who have acquired the habit of experiencing some of their emotions by proxy?[7]

Breaking through falsehood or oblivion – the victim's right to know

"*¿Dónde están?* Where are they?" This is the haunting question which the families of the disappeared never stop asking the authorities in their countries, whether in Algeria, Lebanon, Bosnia, Russia, Guatemala, Argentina, Chile, Colombia or elsewhere.

Wives, parents and children demand to know the truth about what happened to their husband, mother or father, brother or sister who was carried off one day by the police or a paramilitary group and has never reappeared, living or dead. In most cases, family members come up against a wall of silence or lies on the part of the authorities. Fearful of opening the files which would reveal military and political responsibility for the odious practice of causing human beings to disappear, governments claim that they do not know or cannot confirm the truth.

In Latin America, "amnesty" laws imposed by military governments and inherited by the civilian governments went even further by legalizing this refusal to give answers. The darkest periods of repression during which the majority of the disappearances took place have been erased from history, enclosed within walls of silence: "beyond this frontier there is nothing more to know".

"Don't remain fixed on the past, forget about it, look to the future!" This is the authorities' constant message. But for the victims and their families, the answer is No! It is humanly impossible to forget such a crime as the forced disappearance of a loved one. To forget his or her absence – or to accept it without knowing the truth about it – is to become an accomplice to the crime.

> We must keep obstinately in the present, with all its bloodshed and ignominy, the very thing which is already being pushed into the convenient land of oblivion. We must keep on regarding persons as alive who perhaps no longer are, but whose return it is our obligation to demand, naming them one by one until we finally get an answer containing the truth which at present the authorities are trying to evade.[8]

One of the most tragic consequences of the lack of answers about the fate of disappeared persons is that it prevents those left behind from entering into the essential process of grieving. For individuals this often leads to serious psychological problems; and it can sometimes be catastrophic at the collective level. In the culture of many indigenous peoples, for example, paying homage to the dead and giving them a respectful burial is a sacred act which belongs to the basic values of the community. To be prevented from carrying out rites of mourning is an outrage and an offence not only to the immediate family, but also to the entire society.

Guatemala is a case in point. Most of its estimated 45,000 disappeared come from among the Mayan peoples. This essential aspect of the healing of wounds of the wider society was emphasized by the country's Commission on Historical Clarification in its final report, entitled "Memory of Silence":

> Forced disappearance was the most pernicious practice in this sense, due to the uncertainty regarding the whereabouts or fate of the victim... For all cultures and religions in Guatemala, it is practically inconceivable that the dead not be given a dignified burial; this assaults everyone's values and dignity...

The CHC has concluded that the existence of clandestine and hidden cemeteries, as well as the anxiety suffered by many Guatemalans as a result of not knowing what happened to their relatives, remains an open wound in the country. They are a permanent reminder of the acts of violence that denied the dignity of their loved ones. To heal these particular wounds requires the exhumation of secret graves, as well as the definitive identification of the whereabouts of the disappeared.[9]

The right of survivors of atrocities to know extends beyond unveiling the secrecy about the fate of the disappeared and the dead. To overcome the trauma caused by the violence they have endured and the lack of transparency surrounding the circumstances and causes of their suffering, the victims and those close to them need some form of official and public recognition of the facts and disclosure of who were responsible for causing their tragedy. They need to know that each of their personal stories will become part of the shared memory of the nation and that they themselves will be cleared of any accusation and restored to the community.

This does not mean that the pain will disappear, but at least the anxiety and despair caused by official silence or lies can perhaps give way to calm and healing. Even for those who will never obtain justice, access to the truth is an essential element of consolation.

Clarifying history – revealing the truth

Every people has the right to know the truth about past events and about the circumstances and reasons which led, through the consistent pattern of gross violations of human rights, to the perpetration of aberrant crimes. Full and effective exercise of the right to the truth is essential to avoid any recurrence of such acts in the future.[10]

This principle, evoked as a norm in the report on impunity submitted to the UN Human Rights Commission, is far from being written into international law and the laws of individual nations. It expresses an historical necessity which has been taken into account by the numerous investigating bodies and truth commissions which have been established around the world in recent years.

A costly commitment

The will to seek and to reveal the truth about serious human rights violations can imply a very costly commitment, especially when the events being investigated are recent.

The story of the Guatemalan Roman Catholic bishop Juan Gerardi Conedera tragically illustrates this. He was savagely assassinated in April 1998, two days after making public the results of research undertaken by the human rights office of the archbishop of Guatemala for the "recovery of historical memory". The report, entitled "Guatemala: Never Again!", publicly revealed the truth about certain aspects of the massive human rights violations which had bathed the country in blood for over thirty years. It mentioned specific actions and named those responsible for them at the highest level.

For certain persons who were used to having their crimes cloaked in impunity, this proved impossible to endure. They did not shrink from having a bishop assassinated, and have continued their campaign to threaten and discredit the Catholic Church, trying to silence its voice. As of this writing, Mgr Gerardi's assassination has yet to be punished, and every possible subterfuge has been employed to keep light from being shed on it. On the first anniversary of his death, one of the largest popular demonstrations in Guatemala's history called for an end to impunity and celebrated his memory as a martyr for the truth.

Many other less well known witnesses to the truth have met a similar fate. Leaders and activists of innumerable human rights organizations have been assassinated or received death threats, or had their offices looted, ransacked or destroyed solely because they were trying to find out and make public the serious brutalities carried out by the institutions in power. Witnesses to crimes, the families of victims and those who support them have been subjected to the same abuses.

Fortunately, more and more women and men around the world are prepared, on the basis of ethical, religious or social conviction, to face these risks. Beyond revealing the facts, their goal is to educate, to raise awareness and to prevent the repetition of such atrocities. *Never again!*

Never again!

After the appearance of the report, *Brasil, Nunca Mais* – "Brazil, Never Again" – national commissions around Latin America, working under perilous conditions, often with the support of the World Council of Churches, carried out investigations into human rights violations and published reports under similar titles. All have left their mark on the consciences of their societies.

The Brazilian research was carried on secretly for six years under the protection and authority of the archdiocese of Sao Paulo, in close cooperation with the WCC. The final report sent shock waves around the world. It unveiled official documentation gathered by the military dictatorship itself, revealing its involvement in torture and other crimes committed between 1968 and 1979. The report was promptly translated into English so that the rest of the world, particularly the United States, could see what the application of the ideology of national security had meant in concrete terms.

In Argentina, Paraguay, Uruguay and Chile, similar initiatives arose within civil society, resulting in reports which sought out, organized and interpreted the scattered available bits of information on the most serious crimes committed during their own military dictatorships. Each established irrefutable historical evidence of the atrocities committed and of the suffering of the people, exposing the guilt of those directly or intellectually responsible for or implicated in these crimes.[11] The silence was, once and for all, broken. Except for South Africa, no government has yet been bold enough to assume similar responsibility with respect to the behaviour of predecessor regimes.

The truth commissions

This does not mean that governments have remained absolutely silent. In recent years, a number of governments have sought to distance themselves officially from the practices of the past by creating truth commissions to shed light on the past. Commissions of this kind have been set up in Chile, Argentina, Bolivia, Haiti, Chad, Ethiopia, the former German Democratic Republic, Hungary, the Philippines, Uganda and South Africa. Truth commissions have also been set up by the United Nations as part of the peace agreements that ended armed conflicts (as in El Salvador and Guatemala). Often, the mandates of these commissions have been limited as a result of negotiations accompanying the process of return to democracy.

The official goals of these truth commissions can generally be summarized in four points:
- to allow historical clarification of the facts about serious, massive or systematic human rights violations;
- to create a climate for national reconciliation by morally condemning past crimes and abuses and acknowledging the victims;
- to contribute to the education of the population by highlighting the mechanisms which led to the horrors of the past;
- to respond to the victims' need for justice.

The impact of these commissions has differed from case to case and is in any event difficult to measure in the short term. In general, however, it can be said that these goals have only been partially achieved, since the role of these commissions has not included bringing charges against perpetrators. Only in exceptional cases have the names of individual suspects been made public. Their work is sometimes left incomplete for lack of financing (as in Chad, the Philippines and Uganda). In Haiti a report was finished and is eagerly awaited by the population, but has to all intents and purposes been kept secret due to the lack of political will to publish it.

Except for South Africa and Guatemala, such official reports have left in their wake increased bitterness and frustration. Facts have been revealed only in part; crimes and victims are named, but not the criminals; and only selected serious crimes have been taken into consideration (in Chile, for example, torture victims are not mentioned).

Some of these reports have contained recommendations which were then ignored or set aside by amnesty laws. The worst example is that of El Salvador, where the truth commission set up by the UN produced a remarkable report which for the first time officially named the most highly placed persons responsible for crimes against humanity committed during the war. Five days after the report was published, the government decreed an amnesty in favour of all these criminals, nullifying the report's beneficial effects and all the hopes which the commission's work had raised.

The successes, limitations and failures of these commissions merit close analysis in order to draw lessons from them for other peoples in other circumstances. The most fundamental questions to be asked have to do with the contents of the report, the objectivity of the investigations and the degree to which a genuine attempt is made to draw out relationships between truth and justice, and truth and reconciliation.

Truth and reconciliation: two positive lessons for posterity

While there is no universally applicable model for a truth commission, two outstanding examples deserve closer attention: the Truth and Reconciliation Commission in South Africa, which submitted its report in December 1998, and the Historical Clarification Commission in Guatemala, which made its report public in February 1999.

Each of these commissions was set up as part of the peace negotiations which ended in the one case the apartheid regime and in the other a civil war; and each was called upon to deal with a history of over thirty years, with a heavy burden of crimes and violence. In both cases, the basic goal was to favour national reconciliation.

The working methods adopted by the two commissions were very different, but the spirit in which both worked and the considerable impact they had on their respective societies could inspire processes for truth and reconciliation in other parts of the world.

The Truth and Reconciliation Commission in South Africa

However painful the experience, the wounds of the past must not be allowed to fester. They must be opened. They must be cleansed. And balm must be poured on them so they can heal.[12]

Created through political negotiations between the African National Congress (ANC) and the National Party, the Truth and Reconciliation Commission (TRC) was officially established on 26 July 1995 by the National Unity and Reconciliation Act, an extension of the South African constitution which stipulates in its final clause that "the pursuit of national unity, the well being of all South African citizens and peace require reconciliation between the peoples of South Africa and the reconstruction of society".

The TRC was charged with uncovering as much as possible of what transpired in the country from the time of the Sharpeville massacre in 1960 until the inauguration of Nelson Mandela as president on 10 May 1994. The minister of justice, Dull ah Omar, articulated the vision for the TRC in these words:

Instead of revenge,
there will be reconciliation;
Instead of forgetfulness,
there will be knowledge and acknowledgment;
Instead of rejection,
there will be acceptance by a compassionate state;
Instead of violations of human rights,
there will be the restoration of the moral order
and respect for the rule of law.[13]

The National Unity and Reconciliation Act set out the objectives of the TRC clearly:

The objectives of the commission shall be to promote national unity and reconciliation in a spirit of understanding that transcends the conflicts and divisions of the past by:

a) establishing as complete a picture of the causes, nature and extent of the gross violations of human rights which were committed during the period from 1 March 1960, to the cut-off date, including the antecedents, circumstances, factors and context of such violations, as well as the perspectives of the victims and the motives and perspectives of the persons responsible for the commission of the violations, by conducting investigations and holding hearings;

b) facilitating the granting of amnesty to persons who make full disclosure of all the relevant facts relating to acts associated with a political objective and comply with the requirements of this act;

c) establishing and making known the fate or whereabouts of victims and restoring the human and civil dignity of such victims by granting them an opportunity to relate their own accounts of the violations of which they are the victims, and by recommending reparation measures in respect of them;

d) compiling a report providing as comprehensive an account as possible of the activities and findings of the commission... which contains recommendations of measures to prevent the future violations of human rights.[14]

Under the watchword "Truth is the way to reconciliation", the TRC spent two and a half years conducting numerous public hearings to listen to victims and to those directly responsible, or their accomplices, for human rights violations by the apartheid regime. More than 20,000 witnesses were heard. All observers agreed that this painful examination of conscience provided a real catharsis for the entire society. For the first time, victims testified publicly before the whole country (most of the hearings were televised) about the suffering they had endured. Also for the first time, some of the guilty individuals publicly revealed the crimes they had committed, and said why – this was the condition upon which they could request amnesty. Some asked forgiveness of their victims, others did not.

The historical importance of the TRC's work, both for the future of South Africa and for the ethical challenges it raised, is considerable. A great many books and articles have already been devoted to this experience and many more will certainly follow. The effects of this unique process, which involved the entire nation, are as yet immeasurable, and of course history did not stop with the publication of the report.

On 29 October 1998, Archbishop Desmond Tutu, the president of the TRC, submitted its 3000-page report to Nelson Mandela. Although many had hoped that this would be the occasion for a great symbolic act of national reconciliation, it did not prove to be so. The minority white parties called the report a scandal, and the ANC was indignant to see itself implicated in responsibility for cases of torture or mistreatment of prisoners. And the conclusion of the work of the TRC's most controversial committee, dealing with amnesty issues, was still eight months away. All this illustrates how long and complex a process reconciliation is. The process does not end simply by revealing the deeds that impeded national unity in the past and those responsible for them. As former South African Council of Churches general secretary Brigalia Bam told the Second European Ecumenical Assembly in Graz, Austria, in 1997:

> Even after the TRC has submitted its final report, its success or failure will probably only be possible to judge several years later. The implications of the work of the TRC are much bigger than the life span of this Commission. However, what we can say already now is that (a) the South African TRC process is a genuine one, (b) born out of negotiations rather than military or even ideological defeat; it is not a process driven by the victor's quest for either vengeance or justice in the narrow judicial sense of the word; (c) headed by

respected and competent people, many of whom are religious leaders; and (d) its ultimate objectives are truly foundational in the creation of a "new beginning" for South Africa. This is accepted by the majority of South Africans – even those who may be highly critical of specific aspects of the TRC process itself.

The Guatemalan Commission on Historical Clarification

This commission was established within the framework of the Oslo peace accords, signed by the parties to the armed conflict, under the aegis of the United Nations in June 1994. Under the guidance of three experts, one from Germany and two from Guatemala, mandated by the UN, the commission spent 18 months questioning victims and witnesses of human rights violations and consulting a great many sources of information, including certain CIA archives made available by the US government. The goal of this work was

> to clarify with objectivity, equity and impartiality the human rights violations and acts of violence connected with the armed confrontation that caused suffering among the Guatemalan people. The commission was not established to judge – that is the function of the courts of law – but rather to clarify the history and the events of more than three decades of fratricidal war.[15]

The 3600-page report, *The Memory of Silence*, was made public on 25 February 1999. The crowd of more than ten thousand who gathered for the ceremony received the presentation with shouts of joy and tears of emotion. At last the silence surrounding their sufferings had been broken! The great majority of the people had waited a very long time for this moment. Churches, human rights organizations and civil society associations hailed the report as an historic moment of deliverance.

For the first time, an official document, vested with the authority of the United Nations, revealed the extent and the depth of the sufferings endured by hundreds of thousands of Guatemalans. The report did not mince words in exposing the exact causes of these violent acts and indicating who was responsible, both nationally and internationally, for these crimes. While no individual names are mentioned, the categories of people responsible – military, politicians, foreign advisors, guerrilla fighters – are well enough identified for justice to take its course, if the state authorities commit themselves to carrying out the recommendations. It is worthwhile to quote at length from the prologue to the report:

> Although many are aware that Guatemala's armed confrontation caused death and destruction, the gravity of the abuses suffered repeatedly by its people has yet to become part of the national consciousness. The massacres that eliminated entire Mayan rural communities belong to the same reality as the persecution of the urban political opposition, trade union leaders, priests and cate-

chists. These are neither perfidious allegations, nor figments of the imagination, but an authentic chapter in Guatemala's history.

The authors of the accord of Oslo believed that, despite the shock the nation could suffer upon seeing itself reflected in the mirror of its past, it was nevertheless necessary to know the truth and make it public. It was their hope that truth would lead to reconciliation, and furthermore that coming to terms with the truth is the only way to achieve this objective.

There is no doubt that the truth is of benefit to everyone, both victims and transgressors. The victims, whose past has been degraded and manipulated, will be dignified; the perpetrators, through the recognition of their immoral and criminal acts, will be able to recover the dignity of which they had deprived themselves.

Knowing the truth of what happened will make it easier to achieve national reconciliation, so that in future Guatemalans may live in an authentic democracy, without forgetting that the rule of justice as the means for creating a new state has been and remains the general objective of all.

No one today can be sure that the enormous challenge of reconciliation, through knowledge of the truth, can be successfully faced. Above all, it is necessary to recognize the facts of history and learn from the nation's suffering. To a great extent, the future of Guatemala depends on the responses of the state and society to the tragedies that nearly all Guatemalans have experienced personally...

Thousands are dead. Thousands mourn. Reconciliation, for those who remain, is impossible without justice...

With sadness and pain we have fulfilled the mission entrusted to us. We place this report, this "Memory of Silence", into the hands of every Guatemalan, the men and women of yesterday and today, so that future generations may be aware of the enormous calamity and tragedy suffered by their people. May the lessons of this report help us to consider, hear and understand others and be creative as we live in peace.

However laudable these words, the effort to give the people back their "right to know" will take on its full meaning only if the knowledge is really shared, and if the consequences of these revelations are fully accepted by the authorities. Such reports have to be widely distributed, studied and assimilated by the population. Churches are particularly well placed to offer spaces for dialogue and sharing, for reflecting as a community on the contents of these documents and for amplifying them with stories from the lives of persons present.

Governments must also take the recommendations seriously. In the case of Guatemala, pressure will be needed from national and international public opinion to ensure that the work of the commission does not become just one more report to be filed away.

For peoples, as for individuals, hearing the truth means accepting vulnerability as they look at themselves in the mirror of the past. It is understandable that some people try to escape from the destabilizing ordeal of hearing about and accepting the painful or shameful parts of one's own story, of recognizing the evil of which human beings are capable under certain circumstances, of uncovering the perversity of systems of oppression. But those who have worked in truth commissions share the conviction that this "ordeal by truth" is an indispensable stage in restoring broken relationships among individuals, communities and nations, and in reconciling their memories.

Restoring memories

The last years of the 20th century have seen numerous writings on the theme of memory, reflecting the fundamental human need to recover identity. In the context of forms of globalization which crush or stifle specific cultural differences, fragment societies and weaken traditional systems of social cohesion, communities and individuals today are seeking reference points to anchor their identities on a basis they can understand. People turn to memory in the search for elements to help them to situate themselves in the present and to project themselves into the future.

A person suffering from amnesia loses his or her own sense of identity. Similarly, a people that has part of its memory forbidden to it or kept in silence has also had part of its identity amputated. It is through remembering – through memories preserved and passed on – that we identify ourselves in relation to others. Memories either enable us to live and to build a future, or they imprison us in the suffering and humiliations of the past which destroy us and our future.

Everyone's memory is selective. Each of us builds on an interpretation of what she or he remembers, which provides a frame of reference for understanding the world and other people. When the only things preserved in memory and passed on are atrocities and defeats, when memory is weighed down by humiliations and losses, our interpretation of the world will be distorted by an obsession over past injustices and resentment against those responsible for them. Prejudices – the collective demonizing of others – maintains and reinforces these deadly memories and perpetuates the divisions.

The great question for every people and every person who has inherited a heavy load of suffering is *how to avoid being destroyed by memories.* This is not a theoretical question. One need only think of the destructive role played by "poisoned memories" in triggering the violence against those identified as the "others", the enemy, in the Balkans, Rwanda, Northern Ireland and Algeria – to name only some of the most burning current examples.

When the reference points of a society are steeped in such memories and the culture of revenge they engender, it becomes easy to manipulate people and drive them to act on the pretext of preserving their collective identity, be it national, ethnic, racial or religious. Restoring collective remembrance is thus central to work for reconciliation. It is a matter of raising awareness of the destructive capacity of memory, without glossing over painful facts, but drawing lessons from these darkest pages of history in a way that everyone can accept and understand.

Would the inter-ethnic tensions in Rwanda have grown to genocidal proportions if the collective memory of the Hutu community had not been poisoned by the virus of fear and hate and left untended for decades? Could the violence and savagery of the upheavals in the former Yugoslavia have been avoided if it had been possible beforehand to engage in a process of clarification and reconciliation of the centuries-old memories dividing the peoples of this complex mosaic? How are entire peoples to heal their wounded memories, in Sri Lanka, in Liberia, in Sierra Leone, and so many other places after the guns are finally silenced and they have to live together again?

> The measure of our distance from each other in our nations and our groups can be taken by noting the divergence, the separateness and the lack of sympathy in our social memories. Conversely, the measure of our unity is the extent of our common memory.[16]

Few nations of the world have not inherited damaged relationships, whether among communities within the same country or with neighbouring countries. The memories of majority groups and of the communities of those who were originally slaves, immigrants or indigenous peoples, the memories of colonized peoples and of their former colonizers remain separated. Most painful are the memories of oppressed peoples whose conquerors' memories are recognized as the only "official history".

Awareness of and a sense of joint responsibility for how history has unfolded can come about only through the gradual construction of a "shared memory" which does not try to conceal either the victims or the guilty, the crimes or the acts of courage. Only in this way can a process of genuine reconciliation become possible, founded on recognition of each by the other. This is a long-term process. It cannot be accomplished by governments alone, but must involve all the vital forces of the society. Some practical steps can contribute towards this objective:

– rewriting certain history books and introducing new perspectives into the teaching of history, so as to include the memory of "others" and provide a certain relativity in the approach to history which recog-

nizes that reality is always complex, and that the search for truth calls
for skilful discernment;
–   introducing an ethic of respect into the mass communications media,
    to prevent the spread of stories and images which reinforce distorted
    perceptions;
–   education of public opinion to be more critically-minded, so as to
    develop its capacity to resist the manipulation to which it is all too
    often subjected.

Christian perspectives and responsibilities

Whether at the level of searching for or telling the truth, or of reconciling memories, the churches have a fundamental responsibility. Very
often it is to the church that people turn with the burden of their past
wounds. They look to their faith for the strength and courage to survive
and sustain hope, and they expect from their church a listening ear, pastoral accompaniment and a word spoken publicly which echoes their
thirst for the truth. We may thus identify three primary areas of responsibility for churches and Christian communities regarding the challenges
of truth and memory:
–   at the level of theological and catechetical teaching;
–   at the level of pastoral activity;
–   at the level of public witness and action.

Truth and memory

The resources of faith and of the Christian tradition concerning the
essential role of truth are immense. Pilate's words to Jesus, "What is
truth?" (John 18:38), point to a complex question which Christians and
theologians of every generation have confronted. According to John's
gospel, Jesus did not give a direct answer to the insoluble legal question
put to him by Pilate. Nor in fact did Pilate wait for an answer: the evan-
gelist's report that he left the room suggests that his question was merely
rhetorical. Jesus' word about truth to his disciples was on another level;
he offered the way to know the truth: "If you continue in my word, you
are truly my disciples; and you will know the truth, and the truth will
make you free" (John 8:31-32).

Telling the truth, naming one's mistakes, is at the heart of the Christian tradition of confession. It shows itself in steps taken, both personally and collectively, to exclude lies and hypocrisy and to require each of
us not to try to conceal reality from God, from others or from ourselves.

Calls to remembrance are also a consistent element of the biblical
tradition. The memory of the Exodus and their liberation was at the
centre of the Hebrew people's celebrations, and the affirmation of who

they were. In the same way, Christians are called to remember the liberation that Christ has promised to them, as he invites them to celebrate the eucharistic meal: "Do this in remembrance of me."

How does all this resonate in the preaching and the teaching of the churches today?

> Since memory plays such an important role in the phrasing of identity, the over-riding question which needs to be addressed in the context of our contemporary world is how might the activity of remembering become a liberating process rather than a statement of a situation of captivity? Are we condemned to perpetuate our identities-in-opposition, to view each other as a threat?
>
> Throughout the Hebrew scriptures and the New Testament, the people of God are continually being enjoined to "remember" or to "do this in memory of"... The... understanding of "remembering", then, makes of memory-memorial a dynamic process where the past is contemporary. The identity and self-understanding of the community is celebrated, responsibility is accepted, and forgiveness of sin sought.
>
> The reconciliation that results from this way of remembering will be honest and vital, never cheap. Such reconciliation entails recognizing the interdependence of our histories, even appropriating each other's histories, through which each will empower the other to be free. Through the reconciliation of memories a new identity is born.[17]

Throughout the Christian tradition, references to remembrance are always made with a view to reinforcing that which keeps a community alive, that which allows it to live out its identity in an authentic way and to enter fearlessly into relationships with others.

To tell the truth, to hear the truth, to live truthfully, to keep alive life-giving memories, all these messages are at the heart of the Bible. How shall we pass them on as words of life to the world of today, as a source of inspiration and spiritual strength for all those who have to face the risks of fighting for the truth in difficult situations, and for all those who are struggling in the captivity of unhealthy memories which are destroying them?

Healing

Pastoral accompaniment of victims and those around them is another important way for the church to contribute to the work for truth and the healing of memories. This can take individual or community form. For those who have suffered, the most important thing is being able to speak to someone who listens.

We have seen that it is not easy for people to bring to the surface the memories of the humiliations, violence and torture of which they have been a victim or a witness. Churches sometimes offer – and they are called to do so more often – privileged spaces in which a climate of trust and mutual respect is created, allowing these words of suffering, these wounded memories to be shared and tended.

The churches' ministry of healing should take into account these wounds of memory, which prevent individual persons or communities from being reconciled with themselves and with others.

> We must secure the empowerment of victims in pastoral work. It is so important that the victims are agents of the reconstruction of their memories and not the objects of some psycho-pastoral or missionary zeal... This is the key to our future. The wounded are the healers. This is the biblical nature of reconciliation.[18]

Witness

Public commitment to insisting that the truth be told about human rights violations is also a responsibility of the churches, at local, national and international levels. Society expects them, as moral reference points, to speak a clear and audible word – especially during times of great confusion over values, and when the population is exposed to distorted information.

Such witness is risky. Many Christians, both clergy and lay people, have been among those defenders of human rights who have paid with their safety or even their lives for having dared to demand the truth for victims and to expose official lies.

This task becomes all the more complicated in situations in which the violations are committed during conflicts whose opposing communities are defined by their religion or ethnicity. The challenge for church leaders or congregations is somehow to overcome the nationalistic, ethnic, partisan or other passions of their own members, so that the demands of the universal message of the gospel can be heard.

When it comes to reconciliation of memories the churches have a particular responsibility. They have played and continue to play a key role in the formation of historical remembrance. What analysis – and, if necessary, restoration and reparation – are they prepared to undertake with regard to their own memories in order to promote reconciliation?

NOTES

[1] Dietrich Bonhoeffer, *Letters and Papers from Prison*, London, SCM Press, 1971, p. 17.
[2] Paul Ricoeur, *Temps et récit* ("Time and Narrative"), vol. III, Paris, Editions du Seuil, 1985, p. 275.
[3] Charles Villa-Vicencio, "Telling One Another Stories", in Gregory Baum and Harold Wells, eds, *Reconciliation of Peoples*, Geneva, WCC, 1997, pp. 37f.

4 James Cone, as quoted by Dirkie Smith, in Botman and Petersen, eds, *To Remember and to Heal*, p. 101.

5 "Ecrits de témoins, paroles de victimes", Paris, Centre Primo Levi, 1995.

6 Robert Antelme, *L'espèce humaine*, Paris, Editions Gallimard, 1957, foreword.

7 Adbelatif Laabi, quoted by André Jacques, *L'interdit ou la torture en procès*, Paris, Editions du Cerf, 1994, p. 27.

8 Julio Cortazar, *Le refus de l'oubli*, Paris, Editions Berger-Levrault, 1982, p. 15.

9 *Memoria del Silencio,* Guatemala, Commission on Historical Clarification, 1999, p. 28.

10 Louis Joinet, "Issues of Impunity for the Perpetrators of (Civil and Political) Human Rights Violations", E/CN.4/Sub.2/1997/20.

11 For a bibliography, see C. Harper, ed., *Impunity – An Ethical Perspective*, pp. 136-40.

12 Desmond Tutu, *Report of the Truth and Reconciliation Commission*, 1998.

13 Dull ah Omar, in Botman and Petersen, eds, *To Remember and To Heal*, p. 24.

14 Quoted in Geiko Müller-Fahrenholz, *The Art of Forgiveness*, Geneva, WCC, 1998, pp. 85f.

15 *Memoria del Silencio*, p. 12.

16 Richard Niebuhr, quoted by Charles Villa-Vicencio, "Telling One Another Stories", *loc. cit.*, p. 31.

17 Alan Falconer, *Reconciling Memories*, Dublin, Columba Press, 1998, pp. 16-17.

18 R. Botman in *To Remember and To Heal*, p. 162.

3. Justice and Forgiveness

Ethical perspectives and responsibilities

Justice is central to all the complex and interwoven aspects of the struggle against impunity. The successes and failures of the 20th century have taught us that if we truly want to restore relationships which have been shattered by crimes and acts of violence, then we must work for justice. Without justice of a kind which can be recognized and accepted by individuals and communities who have been wounded and humiliated, reconciliation is simply a pious dream.

Victims know that their suffering was not accidental. Usually it has not been simply the result of a moment of social madness or the act of a sick mind, but something deliberate, often part of carefully planned and executed state policies. Ever more insistently, they are demanding that all those who set these policies, made these plans, carried them out or later covered them up be brought publicly to account before a court of law for what they have done.

Visible justice

This need for justice cannot easily be defined in the abstract. Justice must be seen in concrete historical, cultural or religious contexts. Each culture, each civilization has its own values which define what is just or unjust and are often codified in laws.

While the debate between universality and cultural relativity in human rights is a complex one, this does not mean that there are no acceptable and enforceable international standards.[1] Indeed, peoples around the world have increasingly framed their demands for justice in terms of human rights as defined by the Universal Declaration and the growing body of international human rights law.

Justice is sought at two interconnected levels:

– The victims need public recognition of the wrongs they have suffered and need to see those responsible identified, named and held to

account. Many would insist that justice on this level also includes reparations.
– Society as a whole needs laws based on shared values, institutions to manage the rule of law and assurances from the authorities that the law will be equitably enforced.

However, the need for justice goes well beyond the confines of the system of criminal justice. If "right" relations are to be restored among individuals within a community or between communities, many other aspects must be taken into account. Structural injustices which keep rich and poor divided must be eliminated. Economic and social systems which exclude some "for the benefit of the whole" must be reformed. Mutual respect and tolerance, forgiveness and repentance must be elevated to primary social values.

Of course, properly administered criminal justice is essential to the healing of traumatized individuals and societies. Victims and society at large have the right to expect the law to prosecute, try and sentence violators, especially those whose crimes are intentionally or systematically directed against a vulnerable sector of the population. When the justice system fails to respond or exempts certain categories of criminals from accountability to the law, this calls into question the credibility not only of the legal institutions but ultimately of the rule of law itself.

Public accountability: trial by a court of law

In the normal course of events, it is in a court of law that victims' complaints are heard and offenders are given a public opportunity to defend themselves against charges. A properly administered public trial is not a place where victims avenge themselves, but a space in which the authority of the law is interposed between the victim and the violator. For the law itself to have recognized authority, there must be:
– statutes which clearly define both crimes and penalties;
– impartial courts to interpret and enforce the law;
– agreed procedures by which the court determines the facts on the basis of evidence;
– a supporting system to gather relevant facts;
– penalties which correspond to the gravity of the crime.

Courts of law are in fact a means to foster public morality by making visible the consequences of violating agreed codes of social behaviour. Thus punishment has moral significance for individual victims, for the accused and for the public at large. As the French philosopher Paul Ricoeur has put it:

> The victim is publicly recognized as someone who has been wronged and humiliated. This acknowledgment is not insignificant: society declares the

complainant to be the victim and the accused guilty. Such public recognition has an intimate quality having to do with self-esteem, the dignity that corresponds to the moral quality of the human person. Perhaps we may go a step further and suggest that this recognition of self-esteem is intimately related to the grieving by which the wounded soul is reconciled with itself...

The effect of the publicity provided by a trial cannot be over-emphasized as a pedagogical tool for education in equity, and by disciplining the impure desire for revenge.

Ideally one might say that punishment achieves its aim if the sentence, even if it is not accepted, is at least understood by the one on whom it is passed. When the sentence is pronounced, the accused should know that he or she is recognized as reasonable, responsible and accountable as the author of his or her acts.[2]

Criminal justice thus makes an extremely important contribution to the process of restoring broken relationships by:

– restoring the human dignity of the victims in the eyes of society and in their own eyes;
– recognizing the humanity of the perpetrators by affirming their responsibility;
– educating public opinion by affirming the supremacy of the law over vengeance.

The public trial and judgment of offenders also distinguishes between individual and collective guilt. When the perpetrators of crimes are clearly designated, the burden of guilt is lifted from a given group or social collective. This is particularly important in the case of inter-communal conflicts – such as those in Rwanda or the former Yugoslavia – in order to arrest the cycle of offence-resentment-hatred-revenge, which poisons memories and perpetuates group violence. Trials can help victims belonging to one community to distinguish between the ordinary members of the rival community and those who have acted out their fears through violence.

The significance of the trial and condemnation of offenders who have committed such abhorrent crimes as torture, forced disappearances, organized rape, mass killings and genocide goes far beyond simple respect for the law. The actions of the judicial system can mark a fundamental symbolic break with the practices of the past by showing that such crimes will not be tolerated in the future, irrespective of the political or social status of those who commit them. In this sense, the role of the court is to dissuade and prevent the repetition of atrocities.

The more difficult question in the aftermath of conflict or massive violations of human rights is how to respond to the victims' need for justice by bringing the accused to the bar of justice. Who *should* be prosecuted and punished. And who *can* be tried for crimes in often-tumultuous political contexts? What happens when criminals vanish without having been brought to trial?

Who should be tried?

Theoretically, all persons who were involved in planning, organizing and executing crimes against their fellow human beings should be brought to justice and required to give account of themselves individually before the law.

In practice, however, the question is daunting. What can be done when both victims and criminals number in the tens or hundreds of thousands, as has been the case in many recent situations – in Rwanda, Guatemala, South Africa, Cambodia, the former Yugoslavia, the countries of the former communist bloc in eastern Europe, in the two Congos, Sri Lanka, Sierra Leone, Angola, Liberia, Colombia?

No judicial system in the world today would have the capacity of assembling the necessary evidence on such a number of individual cases; and in the most tragic of these situations the legal system itself is in a deplorable state, undermined by corruption and lacking competent personnel. And mass trials with scarce evidence would be a mockery of justice.

Under the circumstances it is obviously necessary to be selective. Jurists and human rights specialists broadly accept the idea of selectivity according to degree of responsibility. The public, too, generally considers this legitimate, provided that the criteria are made clear and public and are based on principles of law and precedent.

Most agree that the first to be called to account are those who actually devised, orchestrated and oversaw the implementation of atrocities. This rule has been applied by the International Tribunals on the former Yugoslavia and Rwanda, and it will also apply for the International Criminal Court when its statutes come into force. Even so, the few examples below illustrate just how complex this task can be in different historical and political contexts.

In Rwanda, faced with the overwhelming challenge of judging the authors of the genocide, the government passed a law in 1996 defining four levels of responsibility for genocide and crimes against humanity. Even so, how was a country virtually without a judiciary, police or other investigative force to assemble the evidence required to select the most serious cases from among the more than 100,000 prisoners crowded into the country's jails on suspicion of the crime of genocide? And how could the release of those not considered among the most serious cases be made acceptable to the survivors when they saw so few perpetrators being brought to trial, and no reliable official process set in motion to tell the truth of the genocide?

In the countries of Eastern Europe after the collapse of the communist regimes the question was not only who should be tried but also what was to be judged. A main difficulty lay in defining criminal responsibility. The systems of repression that operated in those countries lasted for several generations and were built on diluting individual responsibility by spreading it over a wide and complex network of surveillance, control and execution.

Between the extremes of declaring *all* to be guilty and simply drawing a line under the past, governments of post-communist Europe have adopted a variety of measures to come to terms with the crimes of the past. All have been difficult, and most have remained incomplete. Most countries adopted "lustration" laws, banning from public employment people who had held important political responsibilities under the previous regime or whose security service files indicated that they had collaborated with repressive agencies.

To date, no major trial has taken place that might signify to the population a break with the dark days of systematic human rights violations committed by state authorities. In Eastern Germany feelings of bitterness and frustration are now surfacing. "We thought the question of morality in the history of the German Democratic Republic could be addressed through criminal procedures. This has failed." Some go so far as to say that "the search for the perpetrators is hindering the search for the truth".[3] Perhaps the time is not yet ripe; perhaps other measures need to be taken before peoples can face this page of their history in a frank and lucid way that will reinforce national cohesion and reconciliation.

No two situations are alike, but many Eastern European countries seem to have fallen into a similar trap of mixing together those suspected of grave violations of human rights with everyone suspected to have been in collusion, in one way or another, with the communist regime. The courts are not the place to put former systems of government on trial. Still, the "memory work" about which we spoke earlier is needed just as much in this part of the world as in Africa or Latin America. We may hope that the time will come when the crimes and abuses committed in Eastern Europe's recent past can be addressed in an unbiased way by an appropriate form of "truth commissions" or serious historians. As the crises in the Balkans in recent years have shown, Europe is especially prone to falling victim of its own poisoned memories.

Obedience to superior authority

The task of interpreting the degree to which individual members of the military or police and civil servants in general are responsible for violations of human rights has proved particularly sensitive. In Argentina, for instance, the newly-elected democratic government – despite its best intentions to bring the military dictatorship to trial – was soon obliged to adopt a "due obedience" law exempting lower ranks from any criminal responsibility. Human rights defenders denounced this measure as a form of impunity which legalized the acts of men known to have committed grave crimes against humanity (torture, kidnappings, murder and forced disappearances).

The obedience argument, it should be recalled, was the main line of defence of Nazi criminals like Adolf Eichmann. They argued that they had merely followed the orders of their superiors and were not therefore responsible for the consequences of their actions. Mgr Oscar Romero, the Archbishop of El Salvador, was assassinated by the military for having told soldiers that they were not obliged to obey orders which went against their conscience or convictions.

A soldier's decision to disobey an immoral order is often an act of heroism, of which the consequence could be his own death. Is he therefore to be labelled a criminal when he fails to act heroically and refuse such an order? Or is he too to be counted among the victims? Yet while admitting that pressure brought to bear by higher authorities must be taken into account, many consider it ethically unacceptable to apply the obedience argument to excuse those who have executed immoral or barbaric orders. They would argue that the principle of individual accountability before the law of all those who have committed crimes against humanity must be maintained. In practice, there is still a wide gap between moral principle – around which a new international awareness and consciousness is forming – and giving it the force of law.

What is actually possible?

We have seen again and again that the struggle to overcome impunity leads nearly inevitably to the question of what and how much is possible in a particular historical context. What must be done now to repair immediate damage? What might be left to a later, perhaps more propitious time? In the end, irrespective of the competence and integrity of national judicial systems, the answer to these questions depends on the *political will* of the authorities in place and on their political ability to resist the continuing power of those responsible for past atrocities.

The old adage that "justice delayed is justice denied" points to the danger in moving too slowly. But wielding the swift sword of punishment can be equally dangerous to the pursuit of justice. A new government swept into power by military victory or overwhelming political defeat of the *ancien régime* may have both the will and the means to satisfy people's clamour for rapid trials of those who have committed crimes. Their temptation – as history has often shown – is to mete out a form of "victors' justice" in a spirit of revenge.

Where change has come through protracted political negotiations, necessarily the product of compromise, much depends on the balance of power between the new government and the former rulers. In South Africa, as we have seen, political negotiations between the parties led to the choice of a Truth Commission rather than a criminal court. In the Southern Cone of Latin America, the military ceded power to civilian governments only on condition that the armed forces would never be brought before civil courts. In Cambodia, the new government hesitated over bringing those responsible for the genocide to justice as a result of the potential threat still represented by the Khmer Rouge forces. The hesitance of the Guatemalan government to prosecute the authors of crimes against humanity reflected both the authorities' lack of will and a legitimate fear of the retaliatory capacity of the military.

> Justice is all too frequently bartered away for political settlements. Whether in international, non-international or purely internal conflicts the practice of impunity has become the political price paid to secure an end to the violence of ongoing conflicts or as a means to ensure tyrannical regimes change. In these bartered settlements the victims' rights become the objects of political trade-offs and justice becomes, depending on one's perspective, the victim of the means of *Realpolitik*.[4]

Although the contradictions between an ethical approach to the role of justice and the constraints of *Realpolitik* are almost inevitable this does not mean nothing can be done about impunity – or that social healing is a naive illusion. Something *can* be done, both at the national and the international level. Civil society and especially the churches have a crucial role to play in tipping the scales of the existing balance of power in favour of the victims. Increasingly, they are assuming this responsibility. As Juan Mendez suggests, there is a growing consensus that the most serious crimes against people cannot be tolerated nor left unpunished:

> Proponents of accountability have gained a lot of ground... The theme is firmly established in the agenda of all major challenges of our time. A few ideological battles must still be waged, however, especially to overcome the lack of imagination and vision that often passes for prudence and *Realpolitik*. As in the past, it is not enough to insist on moral principles. The international community must acknowledge the political constraints while insisting that everyone look at them objectively and without preconceptions. The most important point is not so much to impose a set of obligations upon democratic leaders, but to find the means by which the international community effectively sup-

ports the efforts made by some of those leaders – and by organizations of civil society – to achieve accountability.[5]

The importance of public opinion in favour of accountability and against the granting of impunity to those who have committed crimes against humanity is underscored by two recent decisions: (1) the adoption in Rome of the statutes for an International Criminal Court; and (2) the issuance by a Spanish judge of an arrest order against the former Chilean dictator Augusto Pinochet. The general's subsequent detention in London, and the decision by the British government that he could be extradited to Spain to face charges was widely hailed by human rights organizations around the world as a major breakthrough and precedent.

Together, these two events may indeed mark an historic turning point, the dawning of a new era when the voices of the victims and their demand for justice will be heard more clearly and the authors of massive human rights violations will no longer be able to hide under the cloak of impunity. But for this dream to become reality, civil society will have to step up pressures at national and international levels. The victims' right to justice will be realized only if such international law and precedent is recognized in national legislation and applied in concrete situations.

The International Criminal Court

The signing in Rome in July 1998 of the treaty accepting the statutes for a permanent International Criminal Court brought to fruition long and arduous decades of work by human rights organizations and specialists in international law. But the adoption of the treaty did not mark the end of the road. For the Court to be established, the treaty, which was signed by 120 of the 160 states present in Rome, must be ratified by at least 60 states; and its legitimacy and effectiveness will depend on its being accepted by all states. Unfortunately, some governments, chief among them the United States of America, rejected the treaty in Rome and sought to limit its scope. The need for an even greater mobilization of public opinion to change mentalities and bring pressure to bear on governments is obvious. In this the churches have a leading role to play.

One of the architects of the treaty, the renowned international jurist M. Cherif Bassiouni, has described the adoption of the permanent International Court as the culmination of a process which began with the Treaty of Versailles in 1920. These 78 years were

> filled with missed opportunities and marked by terrible tragedies that ravaged the world. World War I was dubbed "the war to end all wars", but then came World War II with all its horrors and devastation. Since then some 250 conflicts of all sorts and victimization by tyrannical regimes have resulted in an

estimated 170 million casualties. Throughout this entire period of time, most of the perpetrators of genocide, crimes against humanity and war crimes have benefited from impunity.[6]

Bassiouni traces the roots of the permanent International Court to the decision by the victorious Allies after the second world war to establish an international military tribunal to prosecute individuals for crimes against peace, war crimes and crimes against humanity. Perhaps the best known of these tribunals were the Nuremberg Trials, in which 24 "major war criminals" were indicted and 22 tried. Additional trials in the zones of occupation in Germany of the four allies resulted in the prosecution of more than 15,000 people. A similar series of tribunals and trials dealt with Japanese war criminals. However, progress in establishing a permanent court of this type through the United Nations and the International Law Commission was blocked by the advent of the cold war.

The extensive international media coverage of the tragedies of the 1990s – particularly in Rwanda and the former Yugoslavia – re-ignited the clamour of world public opinion in favour of establishing an international criminal justice system, according to Bassiouni:

> The highly publicized events of the 1990s reminded the world of similar events in the preceding two decades in such places as Cambodia and Bangladesh, as well as many other conflicts and tyrannical regimes which produced a high level of victimization in almost all regions of the world. Many of these events involved genocide, crimes against humanity and war crimes. Yet, shockingly, almost all of those responsible for these crimes benefited from impunity.
>
> This was due in part to the fact that no international criminal justice system existed to which such cases could have been referred and because national legal systems were either incapable, unable or unwilling to deal with such cases... The establishment of the two ad-hoc Tribunals for Yugoslavia and Rwanda boosted expectations that a permanent International Criminal Court should be established. The mobilization of world public opinion through the work of non-governmental organizations has been the main driving force supporting the momentum for [its] establishment.[7]

Such a court will not be a panacea, Bassiouni warns. By itself, it will not eliminate the possibility of repetitions of the type of tragedies the world has witnessed over the past fifty years. At best, it will be

> an effective complement to national jurisdictions with the capacity to deter and punish and thus to prevent some victimization. The International Criminal Court can contribute to the goals of peace and justice, which are inseparable, but it can neither achieve peace nor guarantee justice. Other institutions and the combined efforts of the international community must be mobilized to strengthen peace and achieve justice...

Justice will dampen the lingering embers of vengeance and enhance the prospects of human reconciliation. Without justice political settlements are likely to become only interludes between conflicts.[8]

Justice and reconciliation

Justice – the rule of law, respect for and obedience to the law – is the foundation of democratic society. It is essential to lasting peace within and between societies and nations. For the Christian, however, justice understood in legal terms is a stage on the way to the more fundamental goal of reconciliation.

Reconciliation is a matter of urgency. Paul advised that one should not let the sun set on an injured relationship; Jesus said we should not present ourselves before the table of the Lord until we have reconciled ourselves with an offended brother or sister. Reconciliation is at the same time an ultimate transcendent matter. Jesus became man and bore the sins of humanity on the cross in order that we might be reconciled to God.

Reconciliation is a movement, a process of restoring broken relationships and, beyond that, of re-creating right relationships between individuals and peoples. It does not automatically occur when the judge's gavel sounds. It does not necessarily follow from a confession of guilt by an offender, nor even from a sincere plea for forgiveness. True reconciliation is not content with restoring the *status quo ante,* but represents a radical break with the past. It seeks to heal not just the present rupture of relationships, but also the sources of conflict which were latent in previous, apparently harmonious relationships. Reconciliation fixes its regard less on the past than towards the future. It looks and *moves* forward.

As we have seen, this is not how most transitional governments have approached the matter. Faced with the powerful presence of the perpetrators of past crimes and their supporters, they have often tended to sacrifice or limit justice in favour of order and internal security – to which process they then give the name "national reconciliation". What a perverse distortion!

Restorative justice

Jesus said that he had come in fulfilment of the law, and at the same time to overcome bondage to the law. Reconciliation does not automatically follow from the administration of justice. Many have questioned whether the justice rendered by the international tribunals in The Hague for the former Yugoslavia and in Arusha for Rwanda have in fact advanced reconciliation among the affected peoples. The quality of justice rendered is the critical issue.

Asked whether the power of the Truth and Reconciliation Commission in South Africa to offer amnesty did not in fact lead it to grant impunity to criminals, Archbishop Tutu said:

> We did in fact take very seriously the whole question of impunity... Almost everywhere else the military, before moving out, granted themselves a blanket amnesty. In our case, we said, (1) amnesty is going to be granted on the basis of an individual application..., and (2) amnesty is not automatic... The other condition is, you acknowledge, you accept, you say you are guilty. That's accountability... People have to accept their responsibility for the atrocity they have committed...
>
> The concept of justice that says everybody has got to be punished, the concept of retributive justice, is not the only kind of justice. We believe that there is a restorative justice. The application [for amnesty] is heard in an open hearing, not behind closed doors. Television lights are panned on the applicant..., and that public appearance constitutes a public humiliation..., so if you are looking for punitiveness, there is a punishment. But we didn't think that was where we wanted it to end. We were looking for healing... The purpose is ultimately the restoration of a harmony...
>
> We don't claim that this way of doing things is infallible; it's an option that countries should consider seriously.

"Restorative" justice focuses on rehabilitating the dignity of victims and perpetrators alike, and restoring equitable human relations within communities through efforts for mediation and accompaniment. This concept is gaining ground. For example, the Campaign for Equity – Restorative Justice (CERJ) is an active network in the USA which is working on this approach, encouraging further thinking and commitment, sharing information on different types of initiatives aimed at rebuilding the social tissue within communities. In traditionally communal societies, especially in Africa, efforts are being made to reactivate traditional forms of justice based on recognized and accepted community codes which aim to restore the harmony shattered by criminal acts. In Rwanda, for example, the traditional practice of the *gaçaça* has been revived which relies upon local "wise men" to arbitrate in disputes.

Restorative justice, which seeks to re-create right relations, must take into account the need of reparation for the structural economic injustices that are often at the root of conflict. Agrarian reform and restoration of respect for minority rights are often necessary for long-term processes of reconciliation. Genuine reconciliation requires the removal of the economic roots of oppression and conflict.

Justice and reconciliation are thus intimately connected and their objectives merge. Both bring together individual *responsibility* for others, individual *accountability* to others and the *will to live together.*

Forgiveness

Often those who have suffered violence and humiliation at the hands of other human beings or who have known the death or disappearance of loved ones find it virtually impossible even to think of forgiveness. How can one forgive without seeming to betray one's loved ones? How can one forgive those who refuse to admit the crimes? Who has the right to forgive?

These are not mere theoretical questions. They are the source of anguished soul-searching on the part of the victims and their families – and there is no simple answer to them.

On a recent visit to Rwanda on behalf of the World Council of Churches, I was shocked to hear representatives of some international organizations, funding agencies and even churches insisting on the urgency of forgiveness in order for the country to make a fresh start. Certainly the aim – to rebuild society as quickly as possible – was praiseworthy. But it was being expressed in a way that placed on people who had survived genocide a moral pressure that could only have come from a naive outsider. These appeals for forgiveness failed to appreciate the gravity of the people's trauma and the time they consequently needed to comprehend the depth of the tragedy that had befallen them. For example, at a seminar on the theme of reconciliation organized by a Christian women's association in Kigali, I heard a well-intentioned leader dwell emphatically on the moral and religious imperative of forgiveness. Finally, one woman stood up and, in simple words, raised the question that was probably in the minds of all the victims: "How can I forgive now when no one has come to ask me to forgive them?" Behind her words were other questions: How can you ask us to forgive in the abstract without even knowing what it is that we are forgiving? How can we forgive our aggressors even before they have admitted their crime?

Forgiveness has often been considered to be a private moral and religious matter. The grave conflicts which have overwhelmed us at the close of the 20th century impel us also to consider forgiveness in wider and deeper social and theological terms. Recent studies on the relation between justice and forgiveness, individual and collective forgiveness, God's forgiveness and human forgiveness have explored these depths and offer guidance to those working for reconciliation.[9] A few broad lines emerge.

1. Forgiveness is not a legal category. Forgiveness does not depend on the law and administration of justice, but rather goes beyond these to take into account not only the acts committed against the victim, but also his or her continuing trauma, the lasting consequences of these violations and the victims' relationship with those who have violated them and their loved ones.

2. *Forgiving is not forgetting.* Forgiving does not mean to ignore or erase the wrong that has been done; rather, it requires recognition both of the wrong and of the wrongdoer. In the end, one may be able to forgive the criminal, but one cannot forgive the crime.

3. *Forgiveness is an act of liberation.* In forgiving, the victim decides to free him or herself from the grief and resentment in which he or she is imprisoned. The forgiver does not choose to forget or play down what was done, for it is irreversible, but rather decides not to allow himself or herself forever to be held hostage by the harmful effects of these actions. As Robert Schreiter puts it, "the decision to forgive is the ritual act which proclaims the survivor's freedom to choose a different future."[10] Rather than to suppress the past, forgiveness can free victims and their descendants from the tendency of the past to dominate the present and poison the future.

Hannah Arendt sees the human capacity of forgiveness, along with the capacity to make and keep promises, as the two most important means for profound transformation of human relations:

> The possible redemption from the predicament of irreversibility..., of being unable to undo what one has done though one did not, and could not, have known what one was doing, is the faculty of forgiving. The remedy for unpredictability, for the chaotic uncertainty of the future, is contained in the faculty to make and keep promises. The two faculties belong together in so far as one of them, forgiving, serves to undo the deeds of the past, whose "sins" hang like Damocles' sword over every new generation; and the other, binding oneself through promises, serves to set up in the ocean of uncertainty, which the future is by definition, islands of security without which not even continuity, let alone durability of any kind, would be possible in relationships.[11]

Forgiveness, like justice, is a deliberate choice not to resort to vengeance. Forgiveness, however, goes further. It seeks to speak to the humanity of the one responsible for the forgiver's pain and suffering:

> An act of forgiveness must be understood as a complex process of "unlocking" painful bondage, of mutual liberation. While the perpetrators must be set free from their guilt (and its devastating consequences), the victims must be liberated from their hurt (and its destructive implications). This mutual liberation implies a process of catharsis, and this is the point which scares most people.[12]

4. *The capacity to forgive is a gift.* For Christians, the source of forgiveness and of the human being's capacity to forgive is found in the loving, forgiving God in whom we believe. As Robert Schreiter says,

God's love is what both restores the victim and, in making of the victim a new creation, also makes forgiveness possible.

All this having been said, forgiveness is not made any easier. How does one enter into forgiveness without simply pronouncing the words in a meaningless fashion...? One such way is suggested in the writings of St Luke, reporting the words of Jesus on the cross: "Father, forgive them for they do not know what they are doing" (Luke 23:24).

Before the enormity of the evil being perpetrated, he calls out to God to forgive those that have humiliated him and condemned him to death, reminding us that God alone is the source of all forgiveness. For believers facing the awful decision to forgive or to refuse to forgive, this prayer addressed to God asking him to forgive those who committed the wrong may be the first step that will bring them to grant forgiveness themselves.[13]

It is by trusting in God's power to forgive and to restore the humanity of each and every one that the victims can find the strength and the courage to speak the words of forgiveness that will set them free. It is for them to make the move in faith and in conscience, not waiting, as Dorothea Sölle puts it, for "forgiveness from above", the forgiveness of a God who will settle everything in their stead.

5. Forgiveness is part of the struggle for justice. Forgiveness does not forget the debt but rather *cancels* it. Thus it makes sense only when the debt is identified and recognized by the debtor. Some debts, like crimes against humanity, may be so costly that they cannot be repaid by human justice.

Amnesty – which is related to the word "amnesia" – legalizes forgetting. It erases, in political terms, the wrongful acts and ignores the responsibility of wrongdoers. When politicians equate the granting of amnesty with forgiving, they create an obstacle to genuine forgiveness. The government cannot act for the victims nor offer "forgiveness" on their behalf. Amnesty does not "cancel" a debt; it denies the existence of the debt, which is something else altogether. Confusion about this point is perhaps not surprising, Robin Petersen suggests:

Grace is a notion that is fraught with difficulties: theological, ethical and political. Grace can be and often is spurned; leaving the one who offers it feeling humiliated. Grace can be and often is adulterated into what Dietrich Bonhoeffer called "cheap grace" – the acceptance of the offer of forgiveness and reconciliation without any reciprocal owning of responsibility and action. Bonhoeffer's words concerning this abuse of grace are apposite: "Cheap grace is the preaching of forgiveness without requiring repentance, baptism without church discipline, communion without confession, absolution without personal confession."

If, indeed, grace can be manipulated and abused in the theological and religious spheres, then there is no doubt that the same pertains in the political arena.[14]

Forgiveness, repentance and politics

Forgiveness and repentance, long reserved to theological discourse, are increasingly appearing in the works of political scientists. Philippe Defarges even suggests that "repentance has become an essential component of the spirit of the age".[15] Secular society is more than ever preoccupied with its unhealed wounds, raising the question of the need for collective repentance and forgiveness.

Since German Chancellor Willy Brandt knelt before the monument to the victims in the Warsaw Ghetto, public acts of contrition by politicians for the crimes committed by their countries have become a common element of the political repertoire of statesmen. Governments in Australia, Aotearoa New Zealand and Canada have repented for past mistreatment of indigenous peoples. President Clinton publicly acknowledged the role played by the United States in the repression in Guatemala. Symbolic acts of repentance proliferated in Europe around the commemoration of the 50th anniversary of the end of the second world war. Pressures have been brought on the government of Japan to issue formal apologies for the atrocities committed by the Imperial Government during the second world war in Asia. Jewish organizations demand ever more insistently that European governments not only acknowledge their complicity in the Holocaust, but also pay reparations to survivors and families of the victims.

During the pontificate of John Paul II, the Roman Catholic Church has published more than 90 texts publicly admitting mistakes, failures and historical errors, asking forgiveness, among other things, for its role in the Crusades, the slave trade, the decimation of Indians in the Americas, the Inquisition and the condemnation of Galileo for heresy.

Most of these public acts have occurred in the Judaeo-Christian context. They reflect a new crisis of social conscience. The biblical affirmation that the sins of the fathers will be visited upon their children from generation to generation is increasingly being understood. The past weighs heavily. It cannot and should not be forgotten. People feel the need to be liberated through acts of contrition and repentance in order to turn their attention to a different future. Theological ethicist Donald Shriver has explored this need for "forgiveness in politics" and what a nation requires in order to be able to forgive:

> Forgiveness in a political context is an act that joins moral truth, forbearance, empathy and commitment to repair a fractured human relation. Such a combination calls for a collective turning from the past that neither ignores past evil nor excuses it, that neither overlooks justice nor reduces justice to revenge, that insists on the humanity of enemies even in their commission of de-

humanizing deeds, and that values the justice that restores political community above the justice that destroys it.[16]

What is needed is nothing less than a collective social conversion. In many local communities civil society organizations and churches are already working at this task, but much more time and effort is needed for this to inspire profound change in national policies.

The churches as agents of reconciliation

Central to the mission of the church is reconciliation of individuals with their neighbours, of societies with one another and of humankind with God. Church history is full of examples of martyrdom as a result of selfless obedience to this message, as well as the denial of its demands. Yet this mandate is so central to Christian self-understanding that the churches cannot fail to face up to the challenge it poses in their particular historical contexts.

Believers and the wider societies of which they are a part look particularly to the churches to affirm God's intention for justice to prevail and for relationships broken by sin and evil to be restored. When others fail to run the race to the end – or even to begin it – the church is expected to persevere "in season and out of season", eschewing opportunism, in its witness to society and its political leadership.

To remain faithful to this calling is no easy matter. Political authorities generally prefer that churches attend to the "things of the spirit" – which is often translated as helping people accept the status quo rather than proclaiming the need for justice and reconciliation. Local congregations also shrink from the consequences of "meddling" in politics. More debilitating still, churches are at times divided against themselves along lines of political, national or ethnic loyalties or infected by a desire for vengeance against the "enemy".

How then is the church to remain the church in times of great need: to break the silence, speak the truth in uncomfortable circumstances and proclaim what justice requires and God wills?

The role of women and youth cannot be stressed too strongly. It is often they who suffer the most in times of conflict. Perhaps it is because women know violence so well that they are generally better able than men to reject the idea of vengeance, and are more prone to try to break the cycle of violence. Their will to undertake initiatives to re-establish human relations between opposing groups has been demonstrated repeatedly in the aftermath of many conflicts around the world in recent years. Yet the churches tend rather to marginalize their efforts to mediate disputes and promote reconciliation than to build upon them. Youth are often less bound than their elders to the conflicts of earlier generations, and thus better equipped to build bridges across the gap of conflict in the interest of constructing a new future for themselves and for society as a whole. But they too tend to be kept on the margins of the churches.

How can we recover the vision, the courage and the tenacity to be able to transmit the liberating message of the gospel to men and women who are prisoners of their grief, their desire for revenge, their guilt, their despair? How can we interpret Christ's call to his disciples to be "the salt of the earth" and the "light of the world" in such grievous circumstances?

Ministries to the traumatized

In the vast field of pastoral ministry for justice, forgiveness and repentance among victims of wrong and wrongdoers, the churches have considerable human and spiritual resources to offer.

To be sure, reaching out towards those who have caused the suffering is more difficult and less natural than ministry among the victims. Many of the former probably have nothing to do with the church and do not look to it for anything. But it is also possible that many of them dread the process of truth and repentance to which the churches might lead them.

Repentance is a very difficult act, and most people shy away from it no matter how much they long to be freed from the bondage of their guilt. In the fullest sense, repentance involves admitting all the shameful consequences of one's wrongful act.

> It is more painful still to acknowledge this act in the face of those who suffered it. All confessions of guilt carry with them an element of self-humiliation... To avoid the panic and horror this process of dismantling creates, people go to extremes. They will hold on to denial even if their guilt is there for all to see. They will rationalize their act, play it down or inculpate others... To lay oneself open is nothing less than an act of disarmament. You put down the weapons you employed to dominate others; you renounce the power you gained by stealing it from the victim.[17]

Spiritual and moral accompaniment of those who are ready to open themselves to repentance is essential in most cases. This may happen before the perpetrator has been discovered, to persuade him to present himself in court and so to acknowledge that the law must be equitably applied. More often, it takes place during the period of detention, so that this time of being deprived of freedom can be an opportunity for a person to free himself of his guilt and prepare to be reintegrated into the community. Finally accompaniment is essential after release to allow the return and rehabilitation of the person in the community.

The church must persevere in the fight against impunity and the defence of human rights at every level. As we have seen, this commitment can be risky, for it may clash with public opinion and with the opinions of some church members, who are more concerned about peace and security in the short term than about confronting the powers-that-be who cover their crimes and offences under the cloak of impunity.

Perseverance in commitment to social justice – fighting and redressing the injustices at the root of human rights violations and contributing to the establishment of fair economic relations – is essential to re-creating and renewing relations between individuals and peoples.

In all these areas it is both urgent to act immediately and essential to prepare for long-term engagements. The urgency grows out of the fact that men, women and communities who have been hurt need to see and know that their cry for justice is being taken seriously, even if it cannot be fully met. The long-term commitments are needed because everything to do with restoring relations demands a great deal of time and effort.

Regrettably, there is all too often a call for "action" geared to rapid, quantifiable results. This fails to take account of the spiritual and moral aspects of the processes started by individuals and communities in order to overcome the trauma of the violence they have suffered.

> Too little effort has gone into the existential and spiritual part of the processes of reconciliation: forgiveness, love of one's enemies, restorative justice, re-establishing human relations, healing the churches' internal conflicts, the work of counselling and pastoral accompaniment. Yet it is in efforts of this kind that the "Christian identity" should above all show itself.[18]

The importance and gravity of the situations we have looked at very briefly here – and each of them merits detailed examination itself – call for creative initiatives, the devising of new experiences in the communities and, above all, a renewed commitment on the part of all who want to contribute to justice and reconciliation, not least the churches.

NOTES

[1] On this debate see *Human Rights and the Churches – New Challenges*, Geneva, WCC, 1998 (CCIA Background Information no. 1998/1).
[2] Paul Ricoeur, *Le Juste*, Paris, Editions Esprit, 1995, pp. 199f.
[3] "Une amnistie pour réconcilier les Allemands", in *Le Monde*, 26 Jan. 1999.
[4] M. Cherif Bassiouni, "Searching for Peace and Achieving Justice", *Law and Contemporary Problems* (Duke University School of Law), Vol. 59, no. 4, autumn 1996, pp. 11-12.
[5] Juan Mendez, "Accountability for Past Crimes", *Human Rights Quarterly*, Vol. 19, 1997, p. 282.
[6] M. Cherif Bassiouni, introduction to "For the Establishment of the International Criminal Court in 1998", in *No Peace without Justice*, New York, Feb. 1998.
[7] *Ibid.*

[8] *Ibid.*
[9] Besides the books by Paul Ricoeur *(Le juste)*, Geiko Müller-Fahrenholz, and Gregory Baum and Harold Wells cited earlier, cf. Olivier Abel, *Le pardon – Briser la dette et l'oubli, Paris, Autrement*, 1996; Philippe Moreau Defarges, *Repentance et réconciliation*, Paris, Presses de Sciences Po, 1999; Donald Shriver, *An Ethic for Enemies: Forgiveness in Politics*, Oxford, Oxford UP, 1995; and Robert Schreiter, *The Ministry of Reconciliation*, Maryknoll NY, Orbis, 1998.
[10] Schreiter, *op. cit.*
[11] Hannah Arendt, *The Human Condition,* Chicago, Univ. of Chicago Press, 1958.
[12] Müller-Fahrenholz, *op. cit.*, p. 25.
[13] Schreiter, *op. cit.*, pp. 61-62.
[14] Robin Petersen, "The Politics of Grace and the Truth and Reconciliation Commission in South Africa", in T*o Remember and To Heal*, p. 57.
[15] Philippe Moreau Defarges, *Repentance et réconciliation*, p. 9.
[16] Shriver, *op. cit.*, p. 9.
[17] Müller-Fahrenholz, *op. cit.*, pp. 25f.
[18] Anne Bay Paludan, *Reconciliation in Action*, Copenhagen, Danchurchaid Research Project, 1998.

4. The Prospect of Reconciliation

The prospect of reconciliation is the red thread running through the ecumenical approach we have been examining in the previous chapters. It is the ultimate goal for all societies ravaged by serious violations of human rights, divided by inter-ethnic conflicts or broken apart by war between countries.

The need for reconciliation is in proportion to the wounds caused by the violence. These wounds affect every aspect of life. They concern individuals, ethnic or religious groups, whole nations – men, women and children traumatized to the very depths of their being, communities divided, their perception of "the others" coloured by fear, resentment or hatred. But it is not only human beings and human relationships that are damaged. Moral references and value systems are also shattered. The tendency to "demonize" the enemy, found in most violent conflicts of our time, opens the door to the worst atrocities. Not only are the principles of international humanitarian law ignored, but even the fundamental values of traditional cultures are not respected. Women, children, old people are deliberately made the targets of cruelty and violence. When the aim of the conflict is no longer just to overcome but to humiliate or even eliminate the enemy by means of ethnic cleansing or genocide, there are no longer any values that count.

We have seen that the essential elements for reconciliation – for the healing of wounds, the restoration of broken social relationships, the re-learning of how to live together in peace and mutual trust – are truth, justice, forgiveness and repentance. We have also seen that the demands for truth, justice and reparation are not confined to the legal, political or social domain. The ethical and spiritual dimensions of these struggles are fundamental. There can be no real and lasting reconciliation without re-establishment of the fundamental values that affirm the dignity of every human being and make life in society possible. At this level the churches and religious faiths have a crucial responsibility.

In this book we have tried to describe some of the challenges facing Christians and their churches in this area rather than offering solutions. From this perspective, we may say that the commitment to reconciliation to which we are summoned by our faith requires two things of us:
- being guided by the *vision* of a reconciled human community;
- making that vision a reality by taking *concrete steps* to meet the needs and priorities in each situation.

Reconciliation cannot be imposed by decree. It has to be seen and desired as a vital necessity by the parties to the conflict. This desire for reconciliation, the hope that it is not only necessary but also possible, has to be backed by a broad vision of human relations transformed on a basis of shared values.

Reconciliation cannot be achieved overnight. It must be built up step by step over time, in processes that are neither linear nor automatic, because they are set in the thick of human life, in specific and changing local circumstances.

What is our vision of reconciliation?

One of the most beautiful images of reconciliation in the Bible is that offered by the Psalmist:

> I will hear what God the Lord will speak,
> For he will speak peace to his people,
> And to his saints
> But let them not turn again to folly.
> Mercy and truth are met together;
> righteousness and peace have kissed each other
> (Psalm 85:8-10, KJV).

Clearly, this reconciliation, which is God's plan for God's people, will come in the meeting and mingling of four elements: love (in its dimensions of mercy and forgiveness), truth, righteousness (justice) and peace.

These four themes have recurred throughout this book. When we say that there is no reconciliation without forgiveness, no reconciliation without truth, no reconciliation without justice, no reconciliation without peace, we are indeed looking at things in the widest perspective. But we should not forget that genuine reconciliation involves *all* these dimensions *together* – not one instead of the other, nor one after the other, like steps on a staircase leading up to the goal. This wider vision understands reconciliation as a single and inclusive goal, an ideal to be attained and a promise to be received, with many facets. Some writers associate this vision with the biblical concept of *shalom*.

The images of "mercy and truth meeting" and "justice and peace kissing each other" opens up a vision of reconciliation that identifies both the parts and the whole. Working for reconciliation therefore means promoting through our words and actions, love *and* truth *and* justice *and* peace, all at the same time.

No reconciliation without transformation

Having affirmed this broad perspective, how are we to translate it into practice in the midst of our divisions, our fear of others, our societies characterized by injustice and exclusion?

If human beings are not "to return to their folly" and are to be reconciled with themselves, their neighbours and God, some very radical changes will obviously have to take place. These range from the "conversion of minds and hearts", to the transformation of political, economic and social structures which distort human relations, to the "healing of memories".

Recent experiences have helped us to recognize more clearly the diversities among the situations in which reconciliation is needed. They are set in different epochs, different histories and cultural and religious settings, different political or social circumstances. Each specific situation thus calls for a different process of reconciliation, depending on the nature and extent of the divisions and the wounds, how they are perceived by the people concerned and the political and economic constraints in the given context.

While it cannot be taken as a "universal" model, the experience of the reconciliation process undertaken in South Africa since the end of the apartheid regime is probably one of the most enriching lessons in contemporary history. Nelson Mandela summed up its spirit and method in an article published in the French newspaper *Le Monde* (7 August 1999), of which the essential comments merit citing at length:

> The search for reconciliation has been a fundamental objective in our struggle to establish a government based on the will of the people and to build a South Africa that belongs to all its people. The search for reconciliation was the spur that kept us going through the difficult negotiations on the ending of apartheid and the agreements arising from them. The desire to have a nation at peace with itself is the prime motive behind our programme for reconstruction and development. The Truth and Reconciliation Commission which worked from 1995 to 1998 was likewise an important component in this process... Its work represented a decisive phase in the journey that has just begun.
>
> The path of reconciliation touches all aspects of our life. Reconciliation demands the end of apartheid. It requires us to overcome the consequences of this inhuman system that survives in our behaviour towards one another and in the poverty and inequality which oppress millions of human beings.

Reconciliation is essential for a vision of the future.

South Africans have to remember their terrible past so as to be able to come to terms with it, forgiving when forgiveness is necessary, but never forgetting.

It was inevitable that a task of this scale, so recently started and calling for a process that will take years, would suffer some setbacks. Its success will depend on all sections of our society.

The difficulty of integrating those who have committed serious violations of human rights should not be underestimated... But there are also many encouraging examples of great generosity, mercy and nobility of heart on the part of members of our community.

The best way of making reparation to the victims for their suffering, and the highest recognition of their commitment, is to transform our society into a living image of the human rights for which they fought.

Mandela's words highlight some essential elements to be considered in speaking of processes of reconciliation:

–   At the outset, the desire for reconciliation stimulates commitment and acts as a guide or "spur" for taking the decisions necessary in order to settle the painful heritage of the past. This desire is an essential component in working out a project for a future that will be qualitatively different, not simply a return to the past.

–   Reconciliation is gradually built up by steps that touch and transform all aspects of life – the lives of individuals and the life of the community as a whole. It requires both transformation of the individual behaviour governing relations between people and structural changes in the methods of governance and distribution of resources.

–   Reconciliation is a long-term process. The roads leading to it are long, difficult and tortuous; and there are all kinds of obstacles along the way. Thus working for reconciliation demands perseverance and endurance.

–   Reconciliation cannot come about unless everyone is involved. Any process of reconciliation is by nature inclusive. It must include the past, with its deaths and its suffering (hence the importance of the work on truth and memory); and it must include, in the present, the recognition of the victims and their rights and the reintegration of the perpetrators into society.

–   From the point of view of the victims of human rights violations, the tangible proof that the efforts for reconciliation are more than soothing words and good intentions is the transformation of the society into "a living image of human rights".

When we speak of processes of reconciliation, therefore, we must understand that these are above all processes of transformation – in many cases radical transformation:

- *spiritual and moral transformation* of the individuals or communities which have been divided or at enmity and who decide to mend their broken relations on a new moral basis;
- *political and social transformation* of the structures which have fostered violence and perpetrated injustices within nations or between warring countries, in order to recreate the conditions that make life together possible and, beyond that, to rebuild the foundations of a state governed by the rule of law which guarantees justice and protects the human rights of all its citizens.

No one can be reconciled alone. Reconciliation presupposes the conscious commitment of all the parties that have been in conflict. This is what makes it so difficult, for it involves those who suffered and those who caused their suffering, the victims and the perpetrators. Italian Protestant theologian Paolo Ricca puts the issue well:

> Reconciliation by one-half is not reconciliation. Reconciliation can only be bilateral or multilateral... Forgiveness can be unilateral: I can forgive you, whether you know it or not; whether you accept it or not... but I cannot be reconciled without you.[1]

Experience has proved that no one can be reconciled against his or her will. People who do not want reconciliation cannot be "reconciled" by outside intervention. Violence can be stopped, rules for peaceful co-existence can be proposed or imposed, causes of tension can be reduced, but all these do not yet add up to reconciliation.

Often today we are dealing with increasingly complex internal conflicts, in which there are victims and criminals in both camps and where yesterday's victims become today's criminals and vice-versa. The restoration of relations between the victims and their aggressors and the reintegration of the latter into the national or local community thus pose enormous moral and practical difficulties which should not be minimized and which cannot be overcome simply by good intentions. In his report to the WCC Central Committee in August 1999, general secretary Konrad Raiser emphasized this new moral dilemma:

> How can ecumenical solidarity with the victims of injustice and violence be practised if the distinction between victims and perpetrators becomes blurred; when the former perpetrators become victims themselves? And how can the work of reconciliation begin if both sides understand themselves as victims of injustice?[2]

One element which may help – not by providing an easy answer to these questions, but in finding an entry point to the quest for reconciliation – is distinguishing between the crime and the criminal and between individual guilt and collective guilt.

No matter who perpetrated the violations and no matter what their motives, it must be stated clearly and publicly that there can be no conciliation with the nature of the crimes committed. Apartheid, racism, torture, murder, forced disappearances are *irreconcilable* with Christian ethics and the universal values underlying international law. Evil must be named and condemned. This is an essential foundation for any process of reconciliation.

At the same time, everyone must understand that if a society is to be rebuilt on new foundations, the criminals must not be subjected to the same violence and tortures as they themselves used against their victims. Insisting that the perpetrators acknowledge responsibility for their actions – by admitting to them in public or before a court of justice, for example – is a way of reaffirming their dignity as responsible persons and hence opening the possibility for them to be reintegrated into society and play an active part in reconciliation. It also avoids the situation in which a whole ethnic or religious group is blamed for the crimes committed by a few.

This being said, there remains the difficult question of the attitude of the perpetrators of violations towards their crimes and their victims. Some try to excuse themselves by laying the blame on others; others persist in denying what they did or seeking to justify it; still others simply refuse to talk about it. By rejecting any individual responsibility for the horrors of the past, they exclude themselves from all efforts to correct that past. Unfortunately, this is all too often the case, especially for the intellectual authors and organizers of systematic human rights violations. Society then has no option but to resort to retributive justice.

But for perpetrators who are able to see their crimes through the eyes of their victims, who recognize their responsibilities and accept the consequences, and who are ready to repent, the situation is quite different. Steps for reconciliation are then possible, though it still requires a tremendous effort on both sides to overcome the burden of the past and to agree to work together for a different future.

While any process of reconciliation must be inclusive, as we have said, it is obvious that not all of the people who must be involved in the concrete steps enabling reconciliation have the same expectations or the same attitudes to the undertakings that have to be given. Those who have suffered most from the violence and division, the victims and their communities, are the ones most in need of seeing their personal situations, their relations with others and their societies transformed by the exercise of truth and justice. They are the principal protagonists in any process of reconciliation. Giving them the priority is not incompatible with efforts to include the perpetrators in the dynamic of change. The success of moves for reconciliation will depend on strategies and actions adapted to both groups, according to the historical circumstances in each case.

Ecumenical responsibilities

There seems to be an ecumenical consensus on what Gregory Baum has said: that "the Christian gospel summons the church to exercise a ministry of reconciliation in situations defined by strife and hostility".[3] While the theological arguments for this conviction may differ from one Christian tradition to another, all Christian churches recognize that the mission entrusted to Christ's disciples is to be agents of peace and promoters of love, truth, justice and peace.

In the cut and thrust of human conflicts, however, there is no denying that the response of the churches, their leaders and their members often seems hesitant and inadequate in view of the enormous challenges facing societies which need reconciliation and look to them for moral and spiritual guidance and practical commitment. And many theologians would argue that the concept of reconciliation has in fact been subjected to ambiguous theological interpretations by the churches.

In the first place, the Bible has sometimes been read in the churches in a way that fosters a discourse and attitudes that exclude "others" – those who do not belong to the same religious or ethnic community – from being part of a shared vision of a human race living in solidarity and harmony. Anti-semitism is perhaps the most shameful case in point:

> The church's attitude throughout its history towards the Jewish people symbolizes the church's near-inability to respect the otherness of others. This tragic heritage... has made the church unable to teach its members to respect outsiders, discern among them the quest for the true and the good and search for common bonds of solidarity. Yet this is precisely the spiritual orientation required for exercising a ministry of reconciliation.[4]

Second, the message of reconciliation sometimes proclaimed by church leaders in situations of tension and conflict may sound more like a call for resigned acceptance, a subtle way of stifling the victims' cry for truth and justice in order to obtain a semblance of tranquillity and a return to the status quo. To such half-hearted messages the ancient words of the prophet Jeremiah retain their forceful challenge: "They have treated the wound of my people carelessly, saying 'Peace, peace,' when there is no peace" (Jer. 6:14). In the context of the apartheid which still held sway in South Africa in 1985, the authors of the *Kairos Document* echoed that prophetic indignation: "Trying to persuade those of us who are oppressed to accept their oppression and be reconciled with the intolerable crimes that are committed against us is not Christian reconciliation. It is sin."

A similar note of warning is sounded by feminist theologians and third-world theologians when they stress that the preaching of reconciliation often cloaks a conservative vision of society which refuses to envisage change in the existing economic and social relations and structures.

Wherever we turn in our strife-torn world the tasks of reconciliation are vast and complex. The whole of the ecumenical community is called to engage in fresh theological thinking and courageous and innovative action to respond to the needs of our time. A sense of urgency is needed, not simply as regards the pressure of time, but also in view of the passion and fervour that will have to be brought to these risky undertakings.

There is greater need than ever for input from different theological traditions and experience to enrich Christian thinking and guide the churches' action in this field. To judge from the growing number of books devoted to these issues (see the bibliography), this work has already started. It needs to be enhanced by linking up with the many diverse efforts being made, quietly and anonymously, in local situations.

The experiences cited earlier of the long and difficult paths leading to reconciliation point to some places where the commitment of the churches and of the ecumenical movement can make a difference. They can:

– humbly and perseveringly accompany individuals, communities and leaders who are struggling to come to terms with the heritage of the past, to heal wounds and to work to restore broken relations;

– encourage the creation of spaces for encounter where people can listen and talk to one another and experience new ways of relating to one another on a basis of truth, mutual respect and trust;

– take account of the weight and role of memory as a powerful factor of division, but also as a possible source of reconciliation if it can be freed of the passionate hatreds and myths, handed down from generation to generation, that foment division;

– promote inter-religious cooperation so that religious faiths cease to be used to legitimate or aggravate conflicts and instead offer a moral and spiritual foundation for efforts of reconciliation;

– contribute to the creation or effective functioning of national and international institutions seeking to establish mechanisms that will prevent any repetition of the horrors of the past and to educate the population through truth commissions, courts of justice or the International Criminal Court;

– develop the Christian message of forgiveness and the spirituality that goes with it, comprising the dimensions of truth, justice and peace, which together form the true message of reconciliation.

NOTES

[1] Paolo Ricca, "Réconciliation, reconstruction", *Revue Mission* (DEFAP), no. 71, Nov. 1996.
[2] For the text see *The Ecumenical Review*, vol. 52, no. 1, Jan. 2000.
[3] Gregory Baum, "A Theological Afterword", in Baum and Wells, eds, *The Reconciliation of Peoples*, p. 184.
[4] *Ibid.*, p. 186.